THE THIRTIES IN
VOGUE

THE THIRTIES IN
VOGUE

CAROLYN HALL

FOREWORD BY

DOUGLAS FAIRBANKS jr.

HARMONY BOOKS
New York

Published in the United States in 1985 by Harmony Books, a division of
Crown Publishers, Inc., One Park Avenue, New York, New York 10016.

Published in Great Britain by Octopus Books Limited, 59 Grosvenor Street, London W1X 9DA.

HARMONY and colophon are trademarks of Crown Publishers, Inc.

Manufactured in Hong Kong

Library of Congress Cataloging in Publication Data
Hall, Carolyn.
   The thirties in Vogue.

   Includes index.
   1. Civilization, Modern—20th century. 2. Popular
culture—History—20th century.   1. Vogue.   II. Title.
CB425.H224 1985   306'.4'0904   84-12799

ISBN 0-517-55442-9

10 9 8 7 6 5 4 3 2 1
First American Edition

Designed by STEVE KIBBLE

Contents

FOREWORD

BY DOUGLAS FAIRBANKS JR.
PAGE 6

INTRODUCTION
PAGE 8

THE SOCIAL SCENE:

EDWARD AND MRS SIMPSON
PAGE 20

THE CORONATION
PAGE 24

GEORGE VI AND ELIZABETH
PAGE 26

FACES IN VOGUE
PAGE 28

OUR LIVES FROM DAY TO DAY
PAGE 36

LONDON TIMES, 1936
by Sylvia Thompson
PAGE 42

AT THE RACES
PAGE 46

NIGHTLIFE IN NEW YORK, LONDON, PARIS
PAGE 50

PARIS PANORAMA, 1935
PAGE 56

NEW YORK BULLETIN, 1932
by Cecil Beaton
PAGE 60

PARTIES, PARTIES, PARTIES
PAGE 62

ARTS AND ENTERTAINMENT:

IN THE GROOVE
PAGE 68

MUSIC NOTES
PAGE 70

BALLETOMANIA
PAGE 72

CLENCHED FISTS AND BARE FEET
PAGE 77

RAZZMATAZZ
PAGE 78

SEEN ON THE STAGE
PAGE 82

BOOKS IN VOGUE
PAGE 90

AT THE MOVIES
PAGE 94

A PRIMER OF ART
PAGE 106

SURREALISM
PAGE 108

STYLE AT HOME
PAGE 112

TRAVEL AND LEISURE:

MADAM TRIES HER HAND
PAGE 116

FAR AND WIDE
PAGE 118

UP AND AWAY
PAGE 122

ALL AT SEA
PAGE 126

MAIDEN VOYAGE
by Cecil Beaton
PAGE 128

THE NEW YORK WORLD'S FAIR
PAGE 130

WOMEN SHOULD LOOK BEAUTIFUL
PAGE 132

ABOVE THE SNOWLINE
PAGE 134

UNDER THE SUN
PAGE 136

A HOUSEPARTY
by Cecil Beaton
PAGE 138

DOG DAYS
PAGE 140

NURSERY LIFE
PAGE 142

WAR!
PAGE 144

ADVERTISEMENTS IN VOGUE
PAGE 146

INDEX
PAGE 158

FOREWORD

Photograph by
Cecil Beaton, 1930

The world of the Twenties ended with neither a bang nor a whimper but with a crash. Its echoes continued into the Thirties, but there was still a fashionable group of lucky lotus-eaters, who sought refuge in an escape-world with three headquarters: Paris, New York and London.

The Paris of fine food, wine, women and song – plus Mediterranean extensions – was where the sybaritic foreigner indulged himself to his pocketbook's content. He treated the city as a municipal fairground, with laws applying to its citizens but not to him, where he could call himself a 'Parisian' without understanding the lovely language. But all this – the night-life, Montmartre, the *Folies Bergères*, had been there, it seems, always. Though the 'Gay Paree' of the Thirties rightly boasted of its Cocteau, and its Guitry and its Printemps, of the young Dali and veteran Colette, there was nothing surprising about the continuing Anglo-American preference for Paris editions of the *Herald-Tribune* (including 'Sparrow' Robertson's sports column) and the continental *Daily Mail*, or for the parties of Cole Porter and Elsa Maxwell, for Elsie Mendl, and Maxim's, Charvet, Sulka, Longchamps – with old 'Beau' Barry Wall and his flowered buttonhole, for the Bois at tea-time, Fouquet's and Cartier, or for *haute couture* and Coco Chanel. Only a few new faces were noted, such as Barbara Hutton's and Aly Khan's, and the energetic Señor Rubirosa's.

Perhaps what had once been post-war relief and joy and bubble-blowing had now become the even louder drowning of unacceptable thunderstorms from the east. The enjoyable *chi-chi* atmosphere went on, with its miniature small-talk, its American *largesses*, English Milords and ever-hopeful

White Russians. There was nowhere to be so deliciously, affluently, Coleporterishly bored in as the Paris of the foreigners and the *beau monde* during the Thirties.

New York gloried in its handsome, witty, dashingly corrupt mayor Jimmy Walker. Park and Fifth Avenues dressed up nightly for the blinding lights of Broadway, humming the latest songs by Gershwin, Berlin, Porter and Rogers. They repeated the jokes of Will Rogers and Jimmy Durante, and danced and clapped with Duke Ellington and Cab Calloway and Ethel Waters 'up-town' in Harlem. 'Café Society' (a New York invention) flourished at the Stork Club, at '21' and El Morocco. Rudy Vallee, Bing, Harry Richman and 'Ukelele Ike' sang for us; Paul Whiteman played 'Rhapsody in Blue' and 'An American in Paris'. The great *beaux* of New York – the 'Will' Stewarts, 'Doc' Holdens, 'Jock' Whitneys and their like, who sent their laundry on a round trip to London by Cunard Liner weekly – invited film and stage stars, débutantes and heiresses, society leaders and lesser ladies out to Long Island weekends in their Duesenbergs and Rolls-Royces, driven by liveried chauffeurs. They laughed at Damon Runyon's characters and Dorothy Parker's wit, at Peter Arno's cartoons, and at themselves (in *The New Yorker*). They swooned over Garbo, mocked or loved Eleanor Roosevelt and Shirley Temple, marvelled at each new building to scrape skies, and lionized each new celebrity from any profession – admirable or otherwise.

London in the Thirties still strutted as a 'man's town'. What ever Savile Row or Jermyn Street decided was the vogue for men, Amen! Men of all nationalities boasted of their Scottish tweeds, Irish linen, English woollens, Maxwell's shoes, Hawes & Curtis' evening duds, Lock's hats and so on. . . . No continental stores could equal Harrod's or Fortnum's or Asprey's, and what cars could match a Rolls or a Bentley, or were more stately than the 'Royal' Daimlers? If the white-tied-and-tailed gents and their Parisian-gowned ladies left after their West End play for supper, where but to the Café de Paris? If either of them, on some other night, wished to go revelling, then Ciro's, the Embassy Club, or the Bag O'Nails would do. Or for discreet larking and tightly squeezed dancing in near-darkness, where no one who *could* see would ever even try, let alone tell, there was nothing to beat 'The 400' in Leicester Square. Good behaviour was expected at Court, 'proper' formal clothes were more strictly demanded than ever at Epsom, Ascot, weddings and funerals. The glowing young still chose the right parties to be seen at, and their parents the right gossip to pass on to Chips, or Thelma, or Tallulah, or maybe Freda or even Nada.

Thus did the montage of the Thirties continue, on until the very threshold of the Forties. There was no bang, no crash, no whimper, just the false-alarm wails of air-raid warning sirens. But then unemployment dropped and business improved and this new war was, for the time being anyway, an exciting non-happening.

The Thirties was a wonderful decade, provided one was in the right place. They are, for many, 'the good old days', but so few knew then what to do about them. But whatever was going on in the *haute monde* – whatever was in fashion, or in vogue, was also in *Vogue*.

Douglas Fairbanks, Jr., KBE, DSC

INTRODUCTION

For most people, the Thirties conjures up two distinct images. On the one hand, the Twenties had grown up into a decade of elegance and romance – platinum blondes, white tie, gardenias by your plate and cigarettes glowing in the dark, 'Night and Day' on the gramophone. But Fred Astaire and Ginger Rogers swirling gracefully across the screen were dancing on a volcano. Such Hollywood dreams were an antidote to the fear and anxiety people felt in a period which began with the misery of the Depression and the rise of Fascism and climaxed in world war. In many ways, the people of the Thirties were a lost generation, for whom, as the Cole Porter song went, 'Anything Goes'. Yet their age remains the most stylish and – to use the archetypal word of the Thirties – *glamorous* decade of the century.

For the first half of the Thirties, people struggled with the effects of the Depression caused by the Wall Street Crash. In Britain unemployment rose to three million by 1933; in New York alone it reached one million. In the United States, people stood in breadlines, and tortured themselves in marathon dance competitions, and college graduates – like James Stewart and Henry Fonda – busked for pennies on street corners. In Britain there was the dole and the hated Means Test, and hunger marchers, numbering thousands, converging on London from the Distressed Areas to present their petitions. In answer to the crisis, England came off the Gold Standard, and Labour Prime Minister Ramsay MacDonald formed a National Government.

Even the rich had to tighten their belts. Cecil Beaton, on a trip to New York in 1930, reported: 'One is still grand, but one is poor – the new poor. It is vulgar to be rich and extravagant, and it is in bad taste to give a large party, even if you can afford it. Even if you haven't lost money, you must pretend you have.' In London it was a similar tale. 'Mayfair has gone native,' wrote *Vogue* – no champagne, dinners cut to one or two courses, no canapés beforehand. People closed up parts of their houses, let their servants go and made a thing of serving their own cocktails. *Vogue* ran many articles on how to mix them and arrange drinks trays, and described Chanel's delicious buffet-style meals at her Riviera villa, at which guests found it fun to help themselves and prepare their own salad.

Abroad, there was the growing threat of the dictators. In 1932, *Vogue*'s reporter John McMullin visited Berlin and remarked: 'I am becoming aware of the supremacy of youth in Germany. One feels nothing but youth, the power of youth, and the importance given to youth. There is a *cult* for youth ... Politics is the chief topic of conversation, but ... while there are many parties, they all seem to have one ideal and one desire – to be freed of yesterday. They all seem determined not to suffer for the sins of the fathers.'

McMullin was taken to a demonstration in the Sports Palace of 25,000 young people, most dressed in breeches and black shirts and giving the Fascist salute. 'Is that Hitler, that little man I see? No-one could be more commonplace or more antipathetic. He speaks very badly, he has not a cultivated voice. Why, I ask, is there all this fuss about Hitler? I am told he represents an idea. But I can't find out what idea he represents, for in his speech, he tells the crowd to give him the power, and later he will tell us what he is going to do with it.'

Press censorship meant that nobody really knew what was happening in Germany, although world famous German and Austrian Jews like Max Reinhardt, Einstein, and Freud left their homelands.

At home, Lady Astor's 'Cliveden set' was whispered to be pro-Nazi, and the British Union of Fascists, led by Sir Oswald Mosley, specialized in beating up East End Jews. Mosley's sister-in-law, Unity Mitford, was dubbed the 'perfect Nordic woman' by Hitler; when war broke out, she shot herself. However, many of the British aristocracy were firmly anti-Fascist. Margot Asquith wrote in *Vogue* in 1935: 'We do not believe in mock Mussolinis, silly shirts, self-advertising upstarts. We detest dictators ... Men are tired of force and formula, they ardently desire to follow the things that make for peace.'

Intellectuals declared themselves politically. In 1933 the Oxford Union passed the famous motion that 'This house would in no circumstances fight for its King and country', by 275 to 153. Just three years later, pacifist undergraduates were answering the call for action and going to Spain to fight in the International Brigade against Franco, along with George Orwell, Claud Cockburn, Esmond and Giles Romilly, and Cecil Day Lewis. The Left Book Club, founded in 1936 by Victor Gollancz, Professor Harold Laski, and John Strachey, attracted 50,000 members. Before the end of the decade, many important writers, including W H Auden, Christopher Isherwood, Aldous Huxley, and Louis MacNiece, left the whole sorry mess in Europe for America.

In the main, *Vogue* in the Thirties reflected people's anxious desire for life to be normal despite the gathering stormclouds, and it encouraged its readers to confront hardship and danger with wit and style. Readers were entertained by such writers as Elizabeth Bowen, Harold Nicolson, Ernest Hemingway, Evelyn Waugh, Janet Flanner, Erskine Caldwell, Nancy Mitford, Jean Cocteau and dozens of others. Pierre Roy, Raoul Dufy, Salvador Dali, Giorgio de Chirico, Pavel Tchelichew and Marie Laurencin drew some of the magazine's covers. In 1932, Steichen produced the first photographic cover, a startling and brilliant image of a woman in a bathing suit holding a beach ball, which heralded the end of drawn covers.

As far as *Vogue* was concerned, the best stories featured English

A 'Night in Tahiti' party given by Jean Patou, 1931

titles and American movie stars – 'Diadems and Democratics', as one editorial put it – with the best possible news an Anglo-American lovematch. The Thirties had it all. It was a royal decade, beginning with the marriage of Princess Marina of Greece to the Duke of Kent in Westminster Abbey in 1934. The Princess had lived in Paris with her father and her sense of style and Molyneux clothes made her a fashion icon. *Vogue* published sketches of her complete trousseau. Her favourite colour became known as Marina blue.

The following year, King George V's silver Jubilee was, in *Vogue*'s words, 'a three-ring circus', with at least three events daily throughout the Season. Selfridges spent £10,000 on decorations and one million people came to look. For the first time in history, the police were given permission to carry their lunch, and during the thanksgiving service at St Paul's, which was broadcast by wireless at every street corner, they were allowed to relax for a moment and eat. Some even arranged their hair with pocket combs. C B Cochran, watching over Elsa Schiaparelli's shoulder, said that the parade was timed as perfectly as the best theatrical production – a tribute from a master. By the evening, 'the lid was off', and restaurant orchestras moved into the streets, where the enormous crowds joined in the singing and dancing.

In January 1936 the King died, and Edward, the Prince of Wales, acceded to the throne. His first act as monarch was to fly back to London from Sandringham, which set tongues wagging about his modern ways, for no monarch had ever flown before. The following Sunday he did some gardening instead of going to church. During his father's funeral procession, the gold and sapphire cross on the crown carried on the coffin fell off into the road – an event that was seen as an omen, for within the year Edward had abdicated to marry an American divorcée, Mrs Ernest Simpson.

As Prince of Wales, Edward – David to his family – was the country's playboy Prince Charming. *Vogue* called him 'one of those people who really have glamour'. He endeared himself to his subjects by visiting the steelworks at Dowlais, one of the worst-hit areas of the Depression, and declaring, shocked, 'Something ought to be done'. He left his friend Lady Furness for another American, Wallis Simpson, once divorced and still married to her second husband. Although she was said to be witty and stimulating company, Mrs Simpson looked as starched and prim as a schoolmarm. She was dressed with elegant simplicity by Molyneux, and later by Mainbocher, the American Paris-based couturier and ex-editor of French *Vogue*. It was the perfect story for *Vogue*, but along with the rest of the British press the magazine maintained a discreet silence about the affair, although Mrs Simpson was frequently mentioned in its pages for

Opposite, *Vogue*'s
Coronation cover by
Pierre Roy, April 1937
Left, Mrs Simpson, by
Cecil Beaton, 1936
Above, Princess Marina
by Sorine
Below, Paris welcomes
the King and Queen,
June 1938. Drawing by
R. de Lavererie

her cocktail snack recipes, her immaculate clothes sense, and her jewels, most of the latter lavished on her by the King. However, the foreign press christened her the Queen of Romance, and published outrageous photos of her on a Mediterranean cruise with Edward, with her hand proprietorially on his bare arm.

When it became clear that the King intended to marry Mrs Simpson, 'The Crisis' came to a head. Within a few days of the affair becoming public knowledge in Britain, Edward had stepped down from the throne and left England for exile and virtual oblivion, apart from furnishing copy for gossip columnists and making news with his unwise visit to Hitler at Berchtesgarden. His brother Bertie became King in his place. In 1936, for the only time in its history, England had three kings in one year.

'The Yorks will do it very well,' Queen Mary is reputed to have said, and they did. George VI and Elizabeth and their two young

daughters became the symbol of simple, well regulated, family life. The new King and Queen made a state visit to France in 1938 – Lady Mendl marked the occasion by wearing red and blue in her white hair – and the following year became the first British monarchs to cross the Atlantic. On their arrival in Washington, Mrs Roosevelt's attempts to point out the important landmarks were drowned by the roars of applause from the welcoming crowds. The president's wife, who wrote an amiable newspaper column entitled 'My Day', confessed to her readers her concern about giving the King and Queen early morning tea, and water chilled but not iced. The new King ate hot dogs and drank beer at a barbecue and undid all the harm the Abdication had caused between the two countries – as well as cementing an alliance in the face of mounting German aggression.

Lesser mortals who figured on *Vogue*'s society pages were a rich mix of aristocrats, Hollywood favourites, hotel hostesses, blues singers and tap dancers – 'cafe society', as Frank Crowninshield christened them in the magazine, because they met and mingled in restaurants and nightclubs, or at Elsa Maxwell's famous parties. (Elfine, the waif in Stella Gibbons' *Cold Comfort Farm*, was encouraged to read *Vogue*'s gossip column 'Our Lives from Day to Day' so that she would not be overwhelmed when she met people who lived rather strenuous lives.)

Glamour of another type – that of the movies – also helped people to forget politics. For a start, the new Odeons and Roxy's were fantasy palaces, probably the biggest buildings most people ever entered. The rich, of course, had their own cinemas at home, like Elsie Mendl, who showed films at her Versailles villa every Saturday night. The Great Controversy still raged between partisans of the legitimate stage and the cinema, but the film industry was gaining ground, with newsreels and travelogues as well as feature films. 'Talk is the weakness of the talkies,' lamented *Vogue*, but the movies had beautiful glittering stars swanning around luxurious sets, who could make you forget the awfulness of a script. Many silent stars turned out to have voices like macaws and didn't survive the transition to sound, and Charlie Chaplin could not bring himself to speak. There was colour too: *Becky Sharp* with Miriam Hopkins was the first film in three-colour technicolour, in 1935. *Vogue* published articles on the men behind the English and French film industries – the Europeans were considered more highbrow than their Hollywood counterparts – and went along to watch Douglas Fairbanks filming at Elstree. Graham Greene was successfully sued for $9,800 for being rude about Shirley Temple in the magazine *Night and Day*. The magazine folded soon after.

Working girls lapped up every snippet about their Hollywood idols and *Vogue* showed them how to achieve the smouldering looks of Garbo, Dietrich, Crawford, and other stars with the use

Facing page, Marlene
Dietrich Russian-style,
1936. ERIC
Right, *Vogue*'s Noel
Coward paper doll, 1938
Above, Shirley Temple
by Charlie Chaplin and
vice versa. Below, Joan
Crawford by herself, 1937

VERSATILITY THREE-PIECE SUIT
WITH DETACHABLE SINGING HEAD

ACTOR'S COSTUME WITH HOOFER
ATTACHMENT FOR TAP-DANCING

VOGUE'S OWN PAPER DOLL, BASIC OUTFIT

THE NOEL COWARD PAPER DOLL

WUNDERKIND PLUSH ROMPER
SUIT AND FAUNTLEROY WIG

GLOBE-TROTTER, PALM-BEACH-COMB-
ER'S KIT, WITH STUBBLE TO TASTE

MAN-ABOUT-TOWN ENSEMBLE WITH
DETACHABLE ROYAL INVITATION CARD

PRODUCER'S OUTFIT WITH SCRIPT
AND MRS. CALTHROP ATTACHMENT

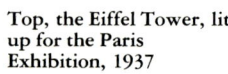

Top, the Eiffel Tower, lit up for the Paris Exhibition, 1937

Above right, the German pavilion at the Paris Exhibition, and above left, the Russian one

of make-up, while they turned their hair as blonde as peroxide would make it. A far cry from the primitive powder and lipstick of the early Twenties, one's battery of tools now included false finger nails and individually applied eyelashes. By 1931, fifteen hundred times as many lipsticks were being sold in London than ten years earlier. Nail varnish came in assorted colours – Woolworth heiress Barbara Hutton wore black – and for a while blue nails, green eyeshadow, and orange lipstick were the rage.

The theatre also flourished, despite the efforts of the British censor, who prohibited anything he considered politically explosive or morally ambiguous. Berlin was the laboratory of Europe, with experimentation in ideas, lighting, effects, and stage settings, but over the decade many of the most important members of Germany's theatrical community left or were expelled from the Reich, including Berthold Brecht and the actress Elisabeth Bergner.

Music fans swooned to the sounds of 'swing'. Benny Goodman and his band, with guest soloists Count Basie and Duke Ellington's trumpeter Cootie Williams, filled Carnegie Hall. 'The thing to do,' explained *Vogue* to readers who did not understand about boogie woogie, 'is to get into a jam session around a phonograph and listen. After a while, if it's in you to be sent, you'll be sent.' To swing, you danced the Big Apple and the jitterbug. But the most popular dance with everybody was the Lambeth Walk, which came from a musical comedy called *Me and My Gal*. It was easy to pick up: you strutted with lifted elbows and bent-in thumbs like the East End costers. Its popularity was sealed in New York when a *grande dame* at the St Regis attempted it with a diagrammed instruction sheet in one hand and a lorgnette in the other.

If you didn't want to go out, the radio entertained you at home. By 1935 there were 600 broadcasting stations in the United States. Buck Rogers, Superman, and – three times a week – the Lone Ranger rode the airwaves, as well as 'good' music, the news, and President Roosevelt's innovation, the 'fireside chat'. The power and potential danger of mass media was sharply demonstrated when CBS radio broadcast a dramatization of H G Wells' *The War of the Worlds*, produced by the 23-year-old Orson Welles. Despite several announcements during the programme assuring the audience that it was fiction, people packed up their belongings and fled in panic, convinced that the Martians had landed at Princeton.

In Britain, the BBC, imbued with John Reith's belief in its public responsibility, gave people what they ought to want, which meant, among other things, nothing but church services on Sundays. In 1932, George V gave the first Christmas message to the Empire. By 1939, 75 per cent of British homes had a radio licence, and could tune in to Arthur Askey on *Bandwaggon* and

Tommy Handley in *ITMA* (It's That Man Again) lampooning the enemy – Funf, the enemy agent with feet of sauerkraut – in his uniquely British way. Radio would sustain the nation during the war, but television was the coming thing. The first television play, Pirandello's *The Man with the Flower in his Mouth* was produced in 1930 for the thirty people in the country who had TV sets. Gilbert Seldes, explaining television to *Vogue* readers, told how in 1932 there were no moving cameras, so that mannequins had to be moved up and down a step ladder in order to show a third of a dress at a time. The first screens were only about nine inches wide, in order to minimize the grain.

England happily embraced not only movies but everything American. 'Mayfair is quite sold on American slang,' reported *Vogue* in 1936, 'and you have only to enter any one of these Mayfair drawing rooms to be engulfed in a spate of transatlanticisms, which describe 'swell guys' as being 'the top' or, its equivalent, 'the Camembert'; 'swell gals' as being 'pretty smooth'; any variety of pleasure as 'easy to take'; while the finer shades of pathos-bathos are now familiar to us as 'sob-stuff' or 'tear-jerkers'. 'Am I right, or am I *right*?' as they would phrase it.' No one used 'amusing' or 'sophisticated' any more; they set you firmly in the Twenties.

Joseph Kennedy was American ambassador to London and made news by refusing to wear breeches and silk stockings at Court. The public was fascinated by Mrs Kennedy's card index on her eight children, which helped her to remember which of them had had measles or been to Europe. Jean Cocteau visited New York and was thrilled by Coney Island and the blackberries and cream he bought from a vending machine, declaring that to eat such food at so little cost, and to buy gardenias for ten cents, was an elegance unknown outside China.

The cult of the open air, first pioneered in the Twenties, had women sunbathing, hiking, and going to nudist camps, although the English climate prevented the latter from seriously getting off the ground. A tan was obligatory, and sports were, according to *Vogue*, 'life's chief pursuit' – although Hitler thought they should be reserved for Aryans and was furious at Jesse Owens' gold medals in the 1936 Berlin Olympics.

Women no longer wanted the schoolboy figures of the Twenties. 'We've discovered our *Bosoms*!' wrote *Vogue*, and the uplift bra from Hollywood ensured people noticed. Joan Crawford-style broad shoulders and mermaid hips in tapering skirts gave women a new femininity. This was achieved by the new Lastex two-way stretch corselette, 'like having a plastic surgeon's slenderizing operation without pain or fee', which fastened with a 'Lightning Fastener', or zip.

What corsets couldn't do, diets did. The decorator Syrie Maugham held diet lunch parties, which *Vogue* found a wonderful

Above, costers doing the Lambeth Walk on Lambeth Walk, and right, Prince Serge Obolensky and Mrs Lewis Tullis dancing it at the New York St. Regis, 1938

idea. 'She decided to devote the first quiet spell London has had since last August to the interests of health and made it known to her friends that any who were feeling the effects of overeating and such a long siege of strenuous partying, could come any day to lunch or dine with her on regime food.' Once Mrs Maugham went on the ultimate diet: 'I starved for six weeks. Yes, literally, for six weeks I ate nothing at all . . . yet I never missed a day's work and feel better than I can ever remember.'

The look was sleek, bandbox smart – epitomized in the extreme by Mrs Simpson, who later, as the Duchess of Windsor, was voted the second-best-dressed woman in the world. 'Today an old boot of a face can win all along the line,' wrote *Vogue*, 'since our present standards demand beauty of figure and finish,

IMPOSSIBLE INTERVIEW:
STALIN VERSUS
SCHIAPARELLI

STALIN: What are you
doing up here,
Dressmaker?
SCHIAPARELLI: I am
getting a bird's eye view
of your women's
fashions, Man of Steel.
STALIN: Can't you leave
our women alone?
SCHIAPARELLI: Look
below you, Man of Steel.
Look at the beauty
parlours and permanent
wave machines
springing up. The next
step is fashion. In a few
years, you won't see
kerchiefs on heads any
more.
STALIN: You
underestimate the
serious goals of Soviet
women.
SCHIAPARELLI: You
underestimate their
vanity.
STALIN: Perhaps I had
better cut your
parachute down!
SCHIAPARELLI: A
hundred other
couturiers would replace
me.
STALIN: In that case,
cut my ropes!

Drawing by
Covarrubias, 1936

rather than mere prettiness . . . If there is any animal today that is the *beau idéal* for female charm it is probably an otter emerging wet from the stream or a chestnut horse glittering with grooming.' Chanel put everyone into simple suits dressed up with dozens of fake gold bangles. Schiaparelli became the most important trendsetter of the decade, grabbing the headlines with her sensational novelties such as her chest of drawers suit, 'shocking pink', edible cinnamon buttons, bustles, black gloves with scarlet fingernails, and mantilla headdresses. But she also created enduring fashions with her shelf shoulders and her dresses with matching jackets, and she pioneered synthetics, including dresses in rhodophane, a sort of glass material. Rayon had come of age, and in 1939 nylon was introduced.

Vogue's photographers, including Man Ray, Cecil Beaton, Horst, Hoyningen-Huené and Steichen, took pictures of models lounging seductively in bias-cut sheath dresses in well-lit Hollywood-inspired sets, often with a cigarette as an accessory: 'a woman without a cigarette has a strange unnatural repose . . . smoking, for a woman, is an adornment, an opiate, a defence, a weapon, a concealment, depending on her inner chemistry.' Everyone copied Marlene Dietrich's grey flannel trousers that were cut like a man's but opened at the side like a sailor's. Sweaters were now high fashion, even – loaded with jewels – for evening. For a time men and women wore the same trousers, watches and sandals, and had the same haircut.

Women continued to take advantage of their expanding opportunities. The magazine encouraged girls to train for work, and dubbed 1932 'the year of the working debutante'. A hitherto undreamt-of physical freedom came with the invention of Tampax. 'George Putnam, who was married to Amelia Earhart, has started a club called Little-Known Husbands of Well-Known Women,' wrote *Vogue*. 'Candidates include Mr Lady Abdy, the Hon Daisy Fellowes, Sir Elsie Mendl and Mr Marlene Dietrich.'

By 1939 there were 2,034,400 cars in Britain, and since 1935 new drivers had had to pass a test. But flying was the big thrill: 'Cars, even the most streamlined, are *démodé*. We fly everywhere as a matter of course,' wrote *Vogue*. You could even cross the Atlantic in the new Pan Am clippers, unless you preferred to go by super-deluxe ocean liner, which was another fashionable thing to do, and gave you the excuse to wear lots of frivolous clothes. The launching of the massive *Queen Mary* in 1936 sent everyone into numeric hysteria over the quantities of rivets and pieces of china and miles of curtains and bottles of wine aboard this 'floating Babylon'.

Travel had become so easy that *Vogue* wrote of weekends in Manchuria or motoring across Sumatra as casually as going to Scotland. But mainly, of course, society turned up on the Riviera – St Tropez was the latest place – or the Lido in summer and St

Top, Hitler's dining room: *Vogue* pronounced it 'German, jumbled and *gemütlich*, a cozy podge of clocks, dwarfs, and swastika cushions', 1936

Above, the flamboyant room at the Villa Torlonio where Mussolini reputedly practised the violin, 1936

Moritz in winter. Surprisingly, despite the political unease, Germany and Austria remained popular holiday spots through the decade. As late as August 1939, *Vogue* ran an advertisement for 'Germany, the land of hospitality'.

Novelties that amused people included the new milk bars, imported from America, all glass, chromium, high stools and counters, which were the rage before the cinema. Backgammon and bridge were popular – *Vogue* reported that Somerset Maugham lost his stammer entirely at the bridge table – and Monopoly, invented in 1936, became a life-saver at country houses when the weather was bad. Activities like pub-crawling ('top marks for spittoons and sawdust on the floor'), watching boxing or motorcycle racing at Haringey, or screaming oneself hoarse at the Arsenal, revealed a certain *nostalgie de la boue*. In 1933 the Loch Ness Monster made its first appearance and had thousands of people dashing up to Scotland to glimpse it.

Art mirrored the events of the real world. In 1933 the Nazis' hatred of modern art closed the Bauhaus school of art and architecture in Berlin, and many of its faculty, including Walter Gropius, Moholy-Nagy, Mies van der Rohe and Paul Klee, left

Above, 'they shelter in the Ritz super-cellars in satin or wool pyjamas by Molyneux or Piguet', Paris, 1939

Right, knitting socks for soldiers: patriotic French *Vogue* cover in red, white, and blue, December 1939

the country. Picasso's *Guernica* first shocked the world in the Spanish Loyalist pavilion at the 1937 Paris Exhibition. Another Spaniard, Salvador Dali, shocked people in a different way, with his pictures of what *Vogue*'s Lesley Blanch called 'bags of offal on crutches'. *Vogue* showed the work of many contemporary artists, including Matisse, Max Ernst, Picasso, Cocteau and Diego Rivera. The New York World's Fair, an optimistic look at the 'World of Tomorrow' on the eve of war, echoed the preoccupation with abstraction in its symbols, the vast geometric Trylon and Perisphere buildings.

Depression or no, skyscrapers still went up. The Empire State Building, 1250ft (385m.) of steel with a mooring atop for airships, was completed in 1931 and immediately came to have a symbolic meaning for New Yorkers. The luxurious Waldorf Astoria, the largest hotel in the world, was opened in 1931 and to Cecil Beaton's delight had telephones in every room.

Literature in the Thirties changed its emphasis from smart and witty novels to stories of trial and endurance. The outstanding bestseller, by an unknown Margaret Mitchell, was *Gone With The Wind*, which sold one million copies in its first six months. John Steinbeck's *The Grapes of Wrath* told the story of dustbowl drought victims seeking a new life in California, and Ernest Hemingway took the Spanish Civil War as his subject in *For Whom the Bell Tolls*. Aldous Huxley's *Brave New World* foretold the horrors of scientific totalitarianism. Elizabeth Bowen, Rosamund Lehmann, Evelyn Waugh and Virginia Woolf gave a vivid picture of what the Thirties felt like in England. Novelist Christopher Isherwood and poet W H Auden wrote an article for *Vogue* on 'Young British Writers on the way up' and included George Orwell, Graham Greene and Stephen Spender in their selection. Books had a colourful new look thanks to the introduction of book jackets, and for the first time you could buy cheap soft-cover copies of novels, brought out by Penguin at sixpence each.

When, in September 1939, Hitler marched into Poland and Chamberlain decided to declare war on Germany, shock and fear were followed by a new purposefulness. In the middle of trial blackouts and air raids, petrol rationing, conscription, and the evacuation of children from the cities, *Vogue*'s policy was 'to preserve the arts of peace by practising them . . . It's your job to spend gallantly (to keep the national economy going), to dress decoratively, to be groomed immaculately – in short, to be a sight for sore eyes.' It encouraged women to work for National Defence and published patterns for dungarees and balaclavas. December *Vogue* was full of presents for soldiers, including silver identity bracelets and food hampers. To begin with, it was a phoney war. People sang 'There'll always be an England', but they knew there was worse to come.

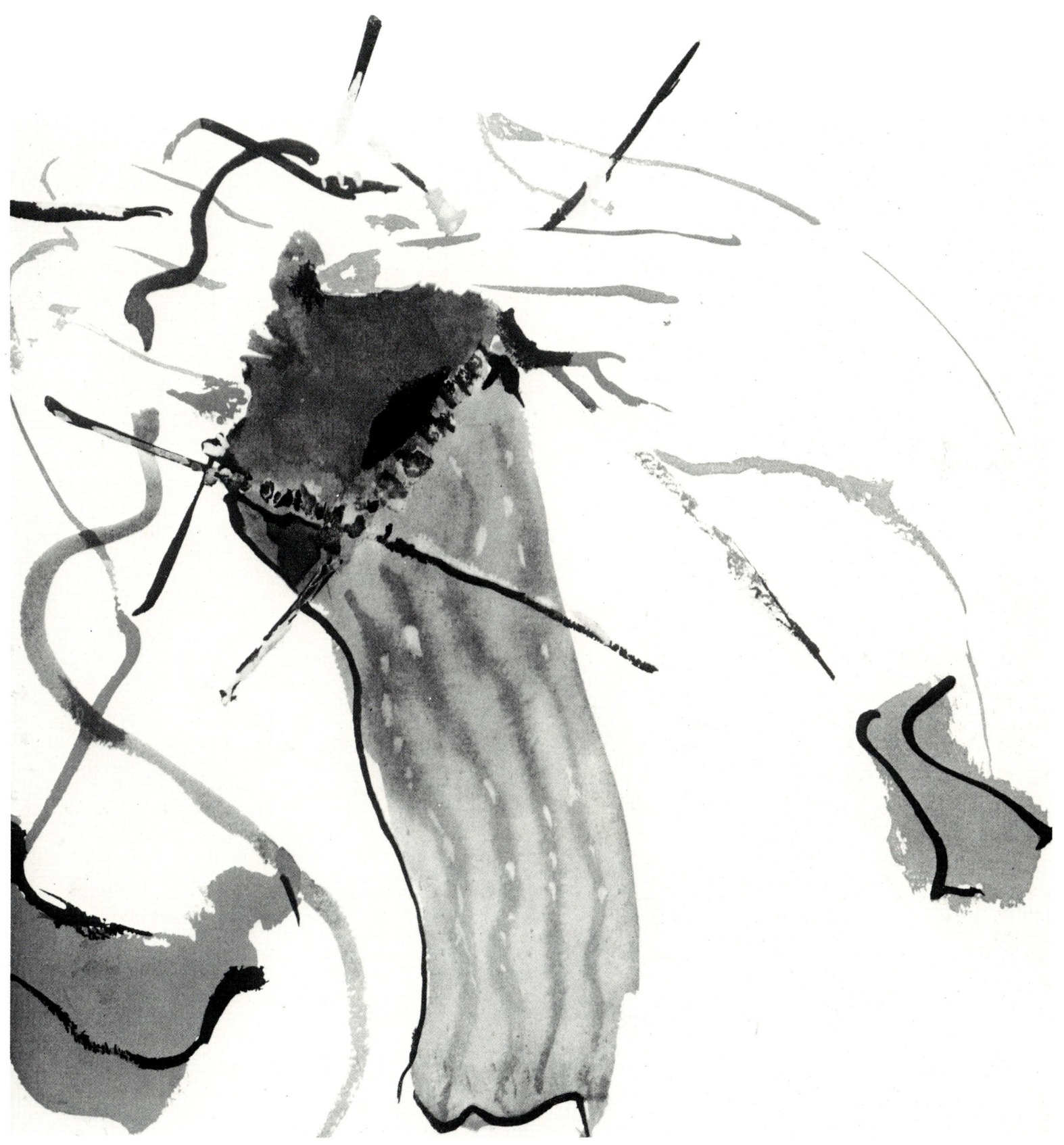

EDWARD AND MRS SIMPSON

It was called 'the love story of the century': it was certainly the scandal of the age, when King Edward VIII stood down from the throne of England after only 11 months – before he had even been crowned – in order to marry Mrs. Ernest Simpson, a brash American from Baltimore who had been married not just once but twice. 'The most alive, glamorous young person in the world today,' *Vogue* called the popular playboy prince on his accession. The world's most eligible bachelor, blond and youthful, spoiled and 40 years old, he was 'first of all a modern'; he dined out, went to nightclubs, and preferred life in Fort Belvedere, a Gothic folly in Windsor Great Park, to the depressingly formal Buckingham Palace. Lady Furness, the former Thelma Morgan and the King's favourite, introduced Mrs. Simpson to Edward and then left him in her care while she made a trip to America. On her return she found the King utterly infatuated by 'Wallis, of all people'. That was what most people thought. Despite her reputation for wit, Mrs. Simpson was smart to the point of severity: she wore her hair parted in the centre in a bun and brushed 'so a fly would slip off it!' And she was a divorcee.

There were discreet references in *Vogue* to Mrs. Simpson as early as 1935, praising her square-cut emeralds and diamonds, her immaculate clothes sense (Schiaparelli and later Mainbocher) and her party fare – 'Mrs. Simpson's food is of such a high standard that the intelligent guest fasts before going to dine or to have cocktails with her'. Her name might appear on the same page as the Prince's, but was not explicitly linked with his. Thanks to Lord Beaverbrook's loyalty, the British press maintained a conspiracy of silence about the affair, although the American papers went to town over the couple's increasingly indiscreet liaison on a yachting holiday in the Mediterranean while Mrs. Simpson was still married to her second husband. As things came to a head, the King's intention to marry Mrs. Simpson and have her crowned Queen at his side precipitated a constitutional crisis: Edward as Defender of the Faith was head of a church that disapproved of divorce, and yet the Queen would have to be crowned during a service of Holy Communion. Prime Minister Stanley Baldwin and the Archbishop of Canterbury

Right, four generations of British monarchs, 1894: Queen Victoria, Edward VII, George V, Edward VIII

Facing page, above left, the Duke of Windsor and Mrs Simpson at the Château de Candé on the day of their wedding, 1937. Mrs Simpson wore a grey-blue wedding dress and a tulle and feather hat, by Mainbocher

Facing page, below left, Mrs Simpson, ignoring the superstition that it is bad luck to be seen in your trousseau before the wedding, poses in a salon of the Château in one of her Mainbocher trousseau dresses. *Vogue* called her 'the quintessence of the modern type – the dressmaker's dream'. CECIL BEATON

Far right, the Duke and Duchess on the balcony of their rented Riviera retreat, La Croë, 1938

impressed upon the King that the country would never agree to this and that he would have to choose between marriage and the throne. On 11 December, 1936, Edward VIII abdicated. He broadcast a farewell speech on the wireless that was relayed by loudspeakers in cinemas and theatres: 'It is impossible to discharge my duties as King as I would wish to do without the help and support of the woman I love.'

Edward's decision led to an estrangement with his family. The Duchess of York refused to receive Mrs. Simpson and Queen Mary called her 'that adventuress'. His friends too fell away.

He and Mrs. Simpson were married at the Château de Candé in France, lent to them by Charles Bedaux, a businessman of doubtful character who later introduced them to Hitler. There were 30 guests – no members of the royal family – and the ceremony was performed by a parson from Durham. Cecil Beaton took exclusive photographs for *Vogue* of Mrs. Simpson in her Mainbocher trousseau in the château grounds and, later, on their honeymoon at Schloss Wasserleonburg in Austria, although most of these appeared only in American *Vogue*. As far as Britain was concerned, Edward's brother Bertie was King, and he was no longer interesting.

Right, Mrs Simpson photographed in the grounds of the Château de Candé, 1937. CECIL BEATON

Below right, the white pillared façade of La Croë, with its green shutters and striped awnings, 1938. The house's practical simplicity, elegance, and dignity, wrote *Vogue*, expressed the joint personalities of the Duke and Duchess. NYHOLM

Left, the Duke's bedroom at La Croë, with heraldic tapestry

Below left, the salon, white with gold columns and bay windows looking down to the sea

Top far left, the Duke and Duchess relaxing under a red and white awning beside the sea at La Croë, 1938

Top centre and top left, informal photos of the Windsors in the grounds of La Croë, 1938. SCHALL

Centre left, the Duke playing with his cairns, Pookie and Detto, 1938

Bottom left, the Duke picnicking with a shooting party at Castle Nikolsburg, Czechoslovakia, 1938

Below, the Duke and Duchess – the latter bandbox smart, even on the beach. 'Her reputation for chic is based upon her great simplicity of dress with an inordinate insistence on perfection of detail,' wrote *Vogue*

THE CORONATION

The pageantry of the Coronation swept away all the upsetting business of the Abdication. The Duke of Norfolk spent 10 hours a day for months working out the order of precedence of entry into Westminster Abbey. Because a Queen was being crowned, peeresses had to bring their coronets as well as tiaras. Many peers hired their robes. When the Countess of Dudley phoned Nathan's, the theatrical costumiers, to hire robes, she was told there were none left. 'You wouldn't let Gertie Millar down, would you?' she asked, falling back on her former stage name. 'Oh Miss Millar,' was the reply, 'why didn't you say it was you?'

It took six hours to get everyone into and seated in the Abbey. Edna Woolman Chase, editor of American *Vogue*, was in her place in the North Transept by 6 a.m., despite the unaccustomed problems of donning feathers, and watched the captive audience below as they listened to a symphony orchestra alternating with organ voluntaries and were escorted to mysterious 'comfort stations' hidden away in the recesses of Westminster Abbey. Peers ate sandwiches hidden in their coronets. One Peer's hipflask burst during prayers. For Mrs. Chase, the most tender and charming moment was the entry of the Royal Princesses Elizabeth and Margaret Rose wearing miniature court trains of purple velvet. The BBC, with 38 microphones placed around the Abbey, relayed the ceremony by wireless to a listening world. Two thousand viewers actually saw the Coronation procession on television, photographed by three static cameras at Hyde Park Corner.

The country joined enthusiastically in the celebrations. London houses were let for £500 a week. It took three seamstresses three days to stitch the GR VI cipher on to the curtains at Covent Garden. Selfridges' decorations so impressed an Indian prince that he bought them lock, stock and barrel to take home. Coronation souvenirs plumbed new depths: you could attain fervid heights of loyalty in a Coronation pinaforette or corset, toast the Royal couple in Coronation Fizz, or blow your nose on a handkerchief scratchily embossed with 'our little Princesses' in contrasting shades. *Vogue* published menus for Coronation dinner parties, and even a gross-point design for a chair-back by Vanessa Bell, exclusive to *Vogue* readers – 'a distinguished memento of the Coronation'.

Right, King George VI and Queen Elizabeth

This page, Coronation souvenirs, including coat-of-arms bedhead, 'Princesses' handkerchief, Abdication tea caddy, and Coronation pinaforette and lampshade, 1937

Far right, Queen Elizabeth, drawn by Beaton for *Vogue*, 1937

Right, tiara'd ladies, top to bottom: Lady Louis Mountbatten, Viscountess Wimborne, the Duchess of Westminster, Lady Brownlow, 1937. CECIL BEATON

George and Elizabeth

On 12 May 1937, the Duke and Duchess of York were crowned King and Queen of Great Britain, Ireland, the Empire of India, and the Dominions beyond the seas. It was considered that there had been too much upset already without rescheduling the date of the Coronation. The country hardly knew anything about the second-in-line prince, 'Bertie', but transferred its affection from Edward to him and his wife and two young daughters with scarcely a hiccup. The new king had always preferred a quiet life out of the limelight and had never been groomed for kingship. He had a stammer, and to begin with there were rumours that he would stand aside in favour of his ten-year-old daughter Elizabeth. But his wife held his hand tightly when he made speeches and gave him confidence.

In complete contrast to Edward's 'modern', night-clubbing image, Bertie and Elizabeth were 'natural, cheerful, and unaffected – a charming parallel, appropriately modernised, to the young Victoria and Albert. The picture of their working together a set of chair-covers in gros point is sure to appeal to some ... future playwright'. The new king's 'Albertian attention to duty' seemed, in view of recent events, 'the only possible note for an exalted kingship, that of an almost ascetic.' The Queen, the ninth of the Earl of Strathmore's ten children, was a commoner, although she could trace her descent from kings. 'Her Majesty has had the best social training known to Woman – to be part of an enormous family enjoying a perpetual houseparty,' noted *Vogue*, praising the Queen's 'happy, harmonious personality' and tactfully conceding her 'an inborn sense of style that triumphs over fashion'.

The spotlight, filtered firmly by her protective mother, also fell on the heir presumptive Princess Elizabeth. Her clothes – classic and conservative – were noted by every conscientious mama in England. *Vogue* discussed her right to be happy as a child – a right never before acknowledged in the schooling of an English queen – her education under a French governess, her talents and accomplishments. She was said to be good at Scottish reels.

Right, the Queen and princesses at Glamis Castle, the Queen's ancestral home, famous for its link with the Macbeth legend, 1937

Top left, Princess Elizabeth (right) joins in a tug-of-war at Balmoral Castle, 1939

Above, the royal family drawn by Rex Whistler, 1937

Top right, the royal family in Scotland, 1938

Right, the thirteen-year-old Princess Elizabeth visits the London Zoo, 1939

FACES IN VOGUE

'Society has relaxed without disintegrating,' wrote *Vogue* in 1934. 'It is not so hidebound, not so careful to include only those of completely similar upbringing.' The cosmopolitan celebrity socialites, whose portraits, photographed by Cecil Beaton, Hoyningen-Huené, Horst, and Steichen, appeared in *Vogue*, reflected this trend. The phrases Jet Set and Beautiful People hadn't been coined yet, but they were it. Prominent through their chic or personality – often both – and always rich, they and their glamorous parties, holidays, clothes, and marriages furnished copy for *Vogue*'s columns and influenced a generation.

Above, Lady Pearson, better known as Gladys Cooper, in 1930, when she was appearing with Sir Gerald Du Maurier in *Cynara* at her own theatre, the Playhouse. EDMUND HARRINGTON

Right, twin sisters Viscountess Furness and Mrs Reginald Vanderbilt, 1932. An escort of the Prince of Wales, Lady Furness introduced him to Mrs Simpson. DOROTHY WILDING

Right, Lady Louis
Mountbatten, wife of a
cousin of the King, and a
chic leader of London
society, 1932. When her
grandfather Sir Ernest
Cassel died, he left her a
vast fortune, including
Brook House on Park
Lane. Lady Louis had it
torn down and a block of
flats erected on the site,
the top two floors of
which became the
Mountbattens' luxurious
penthouse. CECIL BEATON

Far left, Lady Alice Montagu-Douglas-Scott, third daughter of the Duke of Buccleuch, in 1935, the year she married the Duke of Gloucester

Above left, the Countess Haugwitz-Reventlow, the former Barbara Woolworth ('fugitive from a chain-store') Hutton, 1937. At the height of the Depression, in 1932, she had four orchestras and crooner Rudy Vallee flown to her coming-out party. Her manicures, reported *Vogue*, caused a commotion – she painted her fingernails to match her dress. She changed husbands frequently, staying with some of them a matter of weeks. HORST

Below left, Lady Honor Channon, formerly Honor Guinness, wife of Henry 'Chips' Channon, American-born M.P., writer, and socialite. Their blue and silver dining room in Belgrave Square was a replica of that at Amalienburg and cost £6,000. CECIL BEATON

Right, Miss Margaret Whigham of Ascot, 1931. The previous year she was Deb of the Year, and crowds turned up to see her wedding to golfer Charles Sweeny at Brompton Oratory. She is now the Duchess of Argyll. HOWARD AND JOAN COSTER

Left, Lady Oxford, photographed by Cecil Beaton against one of the baroque backgrounds that were his hallmark, 1934. The brilliantly witty and outspoken wife of the former Liberal Prime Minister, Margot Asquith was prominent in London society. She wrote novels and memoirs and contributed articles to *Vogue*

Right, 'the ultra-ultra-ultra in chic', Lady Abdy, 1932. The exotic, Russian-born wife of Sir Robert Abdy, she was over six-foot tall. 'Hers is a rare type that moderns admire enormously,' wrote *Vogue*. She went on to become successful on the stage. HOYNINGEN-HUENE

Far right, above, Lady Mary Lygon. Evelyn Waugh based the Marchmain family in *Brideshead Revisited* on his friends the Lygons. CECIL BEATON

Far right, below, Madame Lucien Lelong, in a suit designed by her husband, 1935. She was the former Princess Natalie Paley, daughter of the Grand Duke Paul of Russia. In 1935 she left Paris to make *Les Folies Bergères* in Hollywood and later remarried. STEICHEN

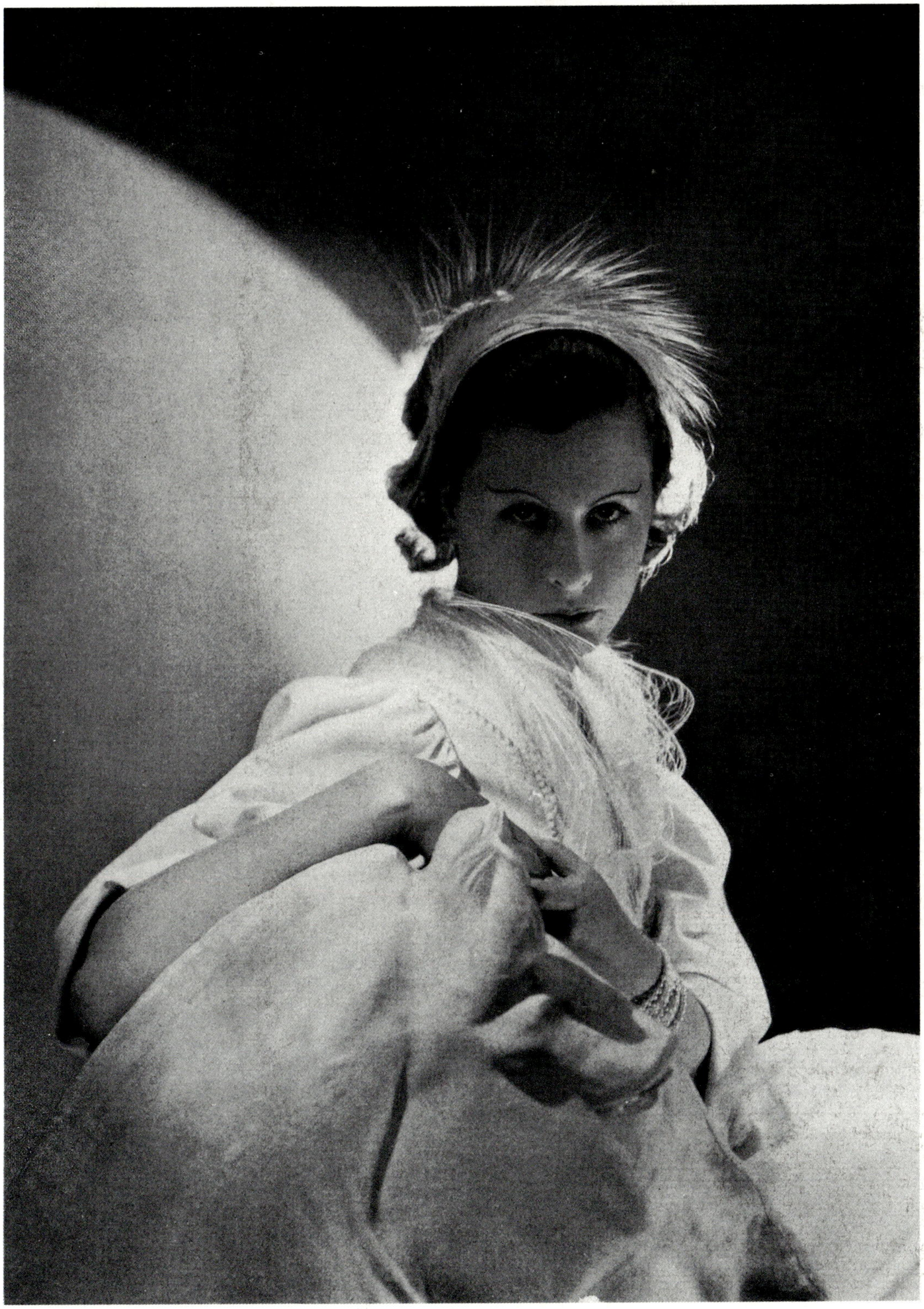

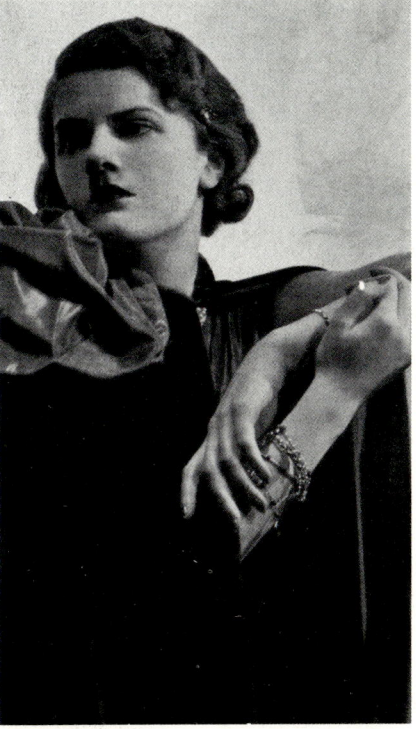

Far left, Mrs Leo d'Erlanger, wife of a merchant banker and the former Edwina Pru of New York, 1932. She was chosen in 1924 as a model for Patou's first American collection. After a brief attempt to make a career as an actress, she worked for a while on *Vogue*. 'Frankly orchidaceous,' *Vogue* called her. 'Her superb Roman-coin profile gives her a strange air of *volupté*, like a Bacchante.' HOYNINGEN-HUENE

Above left, Lady Diana Cooper, youngest daughter of the Duke of Rutland and star of Max Reinhardt's *The Miracle*, 1930. Her large-eyed and ethereal beauty made people stop talking when she entered a room. Her husband Duff Cooper was Secretary of State for War 1935-37 and was first Lord of the Admiralty in 1938 when he resigned over the Munich pact. CECIL BEATON

Below left, the Princess Jean-Louis de Faucigny-Lucinge. The former Baba d'Erlanger, she was prominent in international society and severely chic. During the Thirties she opened a shop in Paris selling nothing but Tyrolean beachwear

Right, Eve Curie, elegant daughter of the scientist Marie Curie, in a dress by Schiaparelli and hat by Talbot, 1937. Her biography of her mother was acclaimed in *Vogue* by André Maurois. After the outbreak of war she made loyal propaganda broadcasts in English and French. HORST

OUR LIVES FROM DAY TO DAY

Extracts from Vogue's diary

March 1931

Nowadays the activities of our friends are not confined within the small radius of Mayfair. Beyond the squalor of Euston, picking up bargains at the Caledonian Market, where almost anything can be bought for a song, you will see Lady Diana Cooper eating chestnuts freshly roasted on a wheel cart. Please don't let's mention the names of those you will see eating ham sandwiches with straw shopping baskets on their arms. Gramophone records are bought from Levey's in Whitechapel; silk stockings in the Berwick Market in the slums behind Shaftesbury Avenue. Chauffeurs are no longer amazed to be told to drive to the lowest dance halls over the river at Lambeth or to the Elephant and Castle. At Charlie's Bar in Limehouse, you will see a lot of bright young people and Lady Eleanor Smith listening to the music of a penny-in-the-slot mechanical piano. The boxing in Whitefriars on a Sunday afternoon is as fashionable as church parade under Achilles's torso used to be before the War. Mrs. Baillie-Hamilton shrieks in the throng, 'Go it Ginger – sock him hard!'

We succumbed to spring fever when Charlie came to Mayfair. Among the hectic impressions that remain of the Pilgrim's Return comes Mr. Chaplin's view of the Four Georges Exhibition, when he looked at the Canalettos of the London he loves, and the polite company tried to concentrate on the glories on the walls. On a sofa sat Mrs. Ronnie Greville. Lady Anglesey was there with her daughter, I saw Lord Spencer, the Duchess of Rutland, Sir

John Reith, Mrs. Baldwin, and Lady Oxford, who took Mr. Chaplin into a window for a talk, while from outside filtered inward the watery sunshine and the last hammerings of the brilliant new Dorchester, which is to have Charles of Claridge's to manage its restaurant. Lady Ravensdale told us of the latest horror threatening us from Russia – the super-loud-speaker at street corners, making the night hideous with propaganda.

October 1931

We wait an hour for the Mahatma in a crowd that is largely Indian, surrounded by those grace-ful women in their saris – black-and-silver one, blue-and-gold another, an orange one, and a daring crimson-and-dark-green. Soft voices, gentle movement, mounting expectation, faces in the windows of houses opposite. Miss Slade is here, looking like an Italian primitive. An Indian student is about to light a cigarette but is stopped by the shocked lady in blue-and-

gold. 'You must not smoke in the presence of the Mahatma.' A shout and we press forward then fall back to make a way for the famous little figure. Then Gandhi, looking very Mickey Mouse, mounts the platform and briefly thanks the Ladies of India while they bring him presents – fruit and a garland for his neck. It is a lovely picture with the illuminated stage and a gentle air of kindly melancholy filling the hall. Madame Naidu, his brilliant friend, is talking to Clare Sheridan who is sculpting Gandhi in his retreat in Knightsbridge in circumstances of some discomfort, as both model and artist must work on the floor.

Mr. H. G. Wells is the pleasantest dinner host in London because he is both charming and easy to his guests. You can talk *with* him. And at Mr. Wells's dinners one is comfortably sure that nowhere else in town is such brilliant talk to be found. We began with vodka and caviare to welcome Julian Huxley back from Moscow. He spoke of communal life to as

Facing page, above left, Lord Berners and Mrs James Beck 'slumming in a Limehouse pub', 1939

Facing page, above right, Lady Oxford, the acerbic and witty wife of the former Liberal Prime Minister, watching the golf at North Berwick with her stepdaughter and grandchildren, 1932

Facing page, below left, the flower shop opened by Lady Diana Cooper in Berkeley Square, drawn by Eric, 1934

Left, watching the boxing at Blackfrairs, 1935

Above left, arriving to dine at the 'brilliant new Dorchester', 1931

Above, Geiger's Hungarian orchestra at Claridge's plays 'the best restaurant music in the world', 1935

perfect a small company of famous individ-ualists as could be gathered in a London flat. Someone suggested an Even Newer Party who would follow Mr. Wells blindly, 'to save us all', but H. G. said he was biding his time, while Charlie Chaplin said he could not talk to crowds. Curious, said someone, when one thinks what a part crowds have played in the success of Charlie. After dinner we all sat talking until midnight when Russian tea arrived, made by our host.

Right, Tilly Losch in polka dots, 1930. CECIL BEATON

Below, Liza Maugham, daughter of Syrie, making news by going hatless, 1935

Facing page, the Sitwell family. Left to right, Sacheverell, Sir George, Sacheverell's wife Georgia, their son, Lady Ida, Edith, and Osbert, 1931. CECIL BEATON

Left, Bea Lillie posing for an article entitled 'How to ruin a good dress', 1931. STEICHEN

Above, Lifar jumping on the piano during an impromptu dance at a Paris party, 1932

July 1933

Syrie's ciré party, as Mrs. Somerset Maugham's brilliant dance might have been called, was a shining affair. We all shone (in the heat), the new dress materials shone, the very chimney pots shone in the glare of flood-lights that were too much for the fuses so that for a time we danced without light but felt familiar figures around us (the Season has thrown us together so that we know one another in the dark). Beatrice Lillie holds up the skirt of her light but long sealing-wax silk dress in the refined manner of 1898. Tilly Losch is just arrived from her ballet in white with green polka dots. Nikitina, in white with a chinchilla slip and a boa-constrictor of organza, has asked (a) for some haddock and (b) to be introduced to Lady Oxford, who is talking to Captain Sitwell (as Mrs. Ronnie Greville calls him). In a corner by the buffet, Mr. Knoblock is telling tales to Lady Pamela Smith, ignoring the waiters who perforce vault o'er them. Next to him is young Mr. Sutro, Society's best imitator, who has a mobile face, sensitive, witty. Randolph *is* enjoying himself! On every sofa in turn. Lifar is receiving congratulations on his ballet as he sits in the sitting-room of Liza's enchanting

Above, 'Austria will be fashionable in August': ladies posing in a victoria, 1936

Above right, the Weisse Rössl Inn near Salzburg, the original of the musical *The White Horse Inn*, 1936

Right, the actress Anna May Wong as she appeared in *On the Spot*, 1931

penthouse through which we pass to reach the cool roof. Back in the supper room we find Anna May Wong, Lady Veronica Hornby (thin-as-a-rail), and Chips Channon with his bride-to-be. He tells me they have taken a (quiet) *schloss* in the Austrian Tyrol. Quite twenty people take me aside and tell me that they too feel they must avoid people by taking a (quiet) *schloss* in the Austrian Tyrol. From which it is evident that Austria will be fashionable in August — reached via Switzerland if you have Strong Views about Germany.

October 1934

The Loch Ness Monster still holds the limelight in Scotland. He has made motoring between Fort William and Inverness the most popular pastime there. But this splendid road is none too wide to accommodate the Monster's public, for one and all drive a zigzag trail with both eyes on the Loch in the hope that he will appear to them (making driving in these parts extremely dangerous). Every few yards along the road people are stationed, camera in hand, patiently awaiting their great moment. He has furnished a strange holiday to many strange people. Beyond a doubt he has really been seen. Seen, yet not seen — for no one has much more to tell than the actual event of his appearance.

January 1936

In Wiltshire there is a bohemian side supplied by the Augustus John clan. The John family give a Vaudeville show every year, in a town near the village where they live. Every member of the very large family (which consists of something like 24 children) has some part in it. They either paint the scenery, dance, or direct. The show is principally dancing because one of John's daughters has organised a ballet school with a great deal of embryo talent. I have never been to anything more fun than the party at John's house after the show. It was the sort of party that only artists can give, for only artists would have arranged it as simply as they did. All the food was in the kitchen. Drinks were put about in convenient places in the house, but you went to the kitchen, got your own glass and washed one if you wanted a clean one. In the kitchen were cheeses, hams, chickens and sausages and you dug into them, cut your own bread and made a luscious fat sandwich to carry off into whatever part of the house your friends were collected. Lady Diana Cooper sat on a sofa with, as usual, a crowd gathered around her. Among them were Lady Juliet and Michael and Joan Duff, Lady Elizabeth Paget, David Herbert, Edward Janes and Olga Lynn.

September 1936

Elsa Maxwell leaves off writing her book long enough to give a party for Grace Moore. She takes over the bathing establishment of the little Garoupe beach, arriving late in the afternoon with forty chickens to be cooked on the spit, cases of champagne and lots of lanterns, wearing a dress with a design of

cornplasters all over it and a yachting cap. She gets on the telephone (which never works down here) orders an accompanist, borrows everyone's manservants, asks another twenty people and, looking out to sea, declares she must have fireworks set off from all the yachts. Then she strides off to Lady Mendl's villa next door to coax the chef to bake potatoes (everyone has developed a passion for them here). Will the party really come off? Yes, and how! The food is perfect, the champagne ice cold, there is music, the lanterns are hung, and even the fireworks go off. But best of all Bea Lillie sings 'Paree' and 'I Hate the Spring' – and makes the party a wow.

Of course we dine again at St. Paul. One does every year. But before that we go (as everyone does every evening) to have a drink at the Carlton, just as one would go to the village post office to hear the latest news. A picturesque note is made by the airmen sitting about – amateur flyers who are supposed to have flown over the Spanish border last night and are going again to-night on secret errands. They won't talk – so of course one doesn't know, which probably makes it more romantic than if one did. Comte Riccio, just back from the Olympic Games in Berlin, tells us of what we have missed. Of the excitement when the American flag and again the Italian flag went up in threes, when on two occasions, first, second, and third place was won by one nationality. The Marquise de Polignac reads extracts from her husband's letters (he is a French delegate to the Games) about the magnificence of the entourage of Goering and Hitler – like royalty.

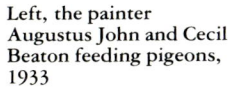

Left, the painter Augustus John and Cecil Beaton feeding pigeons, 1933

Above right, the opera singer Grace Moore, chic in white linen on the Riviera, 1935

Right, Elsie Mendl, renowned party giver, interior decorator, and wife of the British diplomat Sir Charles Mendl, welcoming guests in the garden of her Versailles house the Villa Trianon, originally owned by Marie Antoinette, 1933

LONDON TIMES

Above, the spectators at Lords: 'far, far off, in the centre of that immense green, tiny white figures are playing cricket', 1938

An Eton collage: Left, Lady Forres and her son. Above, an upper boat crew. Right, Mr Doric Bossom with his stepmother, 1938

by Sylvia Thompson, 1936

There is lilac in Berkeley Square . . . and the little hunchback outside Gunter's is selling his usual gardenias to his usual ladies . . . and the suave summer sheep loiter in the green shade of St. James's Park . . . and 'tulle is being worn again' . . . and romantic love is fashionable among very young people . . . and 'Lady Rose-Red is giving a dance at 94 Belgrave Square for her daughter, Miss Rosemary Rose-Red, and her niece, Miss Lettice Coeur de Laitue.'

The King is of Hearts, of Clubs, of Diamonds, and of Spades (for he is supremely the working man's friend and champion); we are all *plus Royalistes que le Roi.*

The debutantes, those Sylphides of the London season, float – an ingenuous, sweet, stately Corps de Ballet – across the lawns of Buckingham Palace, touch the hand of the King, drift and quiver on again to the strain of Chopin, of strawberry ice, of white kid gloves, of cherry pie and roses and antirrhinums.

At Epsom, for the Derby, elegant London, vulgar London, coster London, and half England from Dover to Berwick, are spilled in a basin of green grass. At Ascot you may (once permitted to be there by the Master of the Horse at St. James's Palace) consider yourself, as Jane Austen would have said, 'monstrously genteel', and be photographed wearing a tulle hat and a mackintosh.

If you are the mother of an Etonian, you will spin to Windsor on the fourth of June and eat strawberry mess with your excited and top-hatted progeny; and when the gold light is gone, you will stand beside him in the dark, hay-scented fields and see the sky, above those famous playing fields, ablaze with fireworks. Meanwhile, young love may flit to May Week at Cambridge, to Eights Week at Oxford; and then whirl back again to London, half surfeited with flirtation and hock-cup and lobster mayonnaise.

At Lords, tall, slim, little boys sit by portly dowagers bosomed high, on yellow coaches: and far, far off, in the centre of that immense green, tiny white figures are playing cricket.

And at Henley, the punts drift, clamped together, on the sun-flashing river. 'Regatta' is the name of this ballet – so blue-aired, so white-flannelled. Bronzed profiles, straw hats, picnic baskets, a myriad little coloured flags.

'At Covent Garden, the boxes are filled with Faces and Forearms: gloved and glittering Forearms and Faces strangely glamorous, having the far-away bright arrogance of angels', 1939

The Boats skim and rocket past, and cheering shakes the blue air and the festive sunshine.

At Covent Garden, the boxes are filled with Faces and Forearms: gloved and glittering Forearms and Faces strangely glamorous, having the far-away bright arrogance of angels. (Do not then look for these same faces in the foyer, and meet your Blessed Damozel, tired-eyed, hard-lipped, drinking a gin-and-tonic, and scratching her head to ease her tiara, and your pale-wreathed Beatrice, freckled and talking in her thin English jabber about the performance of her new Bentley.) Between *entr'actes*, there are *Aïda, Tosca, Rigoletto* – Bellezza conducting; Wagner in full force, conducted by Beecham.

Afterwards, since no one has discovered any way to organize the traffic outside Covent Garden, the tiaras, the wreaths, the waistcoats, the gardenias, stand embattled under the vast dim-lit mustard-yellow portico, hoping for their cars, praying for taxis, alter-

nately bribing, beguiling, and reviling the Olympian and indifferent commissionnaires. But, if you care to, you may slip out of this stampede for vehicles and find yourself the only human being beneath the gigantic shadowy arches of the market, and no other living thing there but flowers. For the flower-market has a still, huge fragrant night-life of its own, and you may walk endlessly at midnight between serried banks of sweet peas, of carnations, of lilies, of marigolds, or portly peonies.

Fokine is with the Ballets de Monte Carlo at the Alhambra. *Pride and Prejudice* exquisitely upholstered by Rex Whistler is at the St. James's. Dodie Smith goes on *Calling it a Day* week after week at the Globe. Max Beerbohm's *Happy Hypocrite* is being represented by Ivor Novello at His Majesty's; and the Whiteoaks family are overcrowding the Little Theatre. And every *Tonight at 8.30*, the London which has made Coward crowds to see his triple bill.

'This,' says Coward drama to them, to the Sylphides, to the dangerously-in-love young men, to Lady Rose-Red, and her daughters, 'this is what you are like!' And they come away slipping cloaks about them, furs about them, jerking down white waistcoats, and thinking . . . 'we are wittier and more sensitive, more

desperate, and more elegant in soul than we'd quite realized.'

At supper at the Savoy, the smoked haddock changes its name nightly. Haddock Aïda, Haddock Don Giovanni. Tables crowd each other. Celebrities crowd each other. On a good night, you can't see the food for the stars.

The Sylphides have drifted into fluttering, billowing groups, serene-eyed, bright-haired, with complexions like apple-blossoms, doing a *pas de trois*, a *pas de deux*, in the ballrooms of the solid, tranquil, yet festive London houses. The doors are wide open; and there are red carpets across the pavements of Grosvenor Square, of Mount Street, of St. James's Square.

Above, far left, Noel Coward autographing programmes.
CECIL BEATON

Below, far left, 'Lobster mayonnaise twice—and step on it', 1939.
FRANCIS MARSHALL

Left, dancing at the Savoy

Right, 'The hostess has stood long enough at the top of the staircase, receiving, receiving . . .', 1936

The couples drift up and down the staircase to supper, to the garden, to the conservatories full of hydrangeas and zinnias. The hostess has stood long enough at the top of her staircase receiving, receiving . . . shaking hands and smiling and nodding, while the stream of guests comes up and up the staircase, and the butler's voice booms on, and the band in the ballroom is playing a waltz.

The motors glide from the red carpet in Grosvenor Square to the red carpet (there is an awning there) in Portland Place. From Portland Place to the Embassy, the Berkeley, the Casino, the San Marco, the Blue Train . . .

The night is scented with lilac, with petrol, with lime-trees; and Romantic Love is very sweet and disturbing and glamorous.

AT THE RACES

Ascot is London's crowning (social) glory, the very summit of summer joys, where, convenient to the town, is the *rond-point* at which all circles meet and all paths cross. What Every Young Man Should Know is that though Ascot is (almost) won on the platforms of Waterloo, it is Bad Form to pin the precious Order of Enclosure to one's lapels until the magic lawn is in sight. To show in the train that famous badge – 'the coveted piece of pasteboard' – is a serious error of taste. Behold us then in our white toppers, morning coats and grey waistcoats, waiting for the women (who are always nearly-too-late) beside the impatient race special. From a far platform arriving Americans rub their eyes in wonder and cry, 'So this is England!' For our platform presents a dazzling spectacle. The women are even more beautiful than the men, who are each adorned by a pink carnation. We are off, and after some bright and tiring talk we relax into the only rest we shall get for many hours. Ascot is the most tiring, and physically – and for some

emotionally – exhausting of all our 'events'.

Arrived at Ascot, we leave the train which is carried off by a thoughtful railway company to sit in the sun on a siding all day so as to give us a warm, if stuffy, welcome on our return. In a few moments we are at the Gate of Heartburnings, where eagle eyes are apparently satisfied by a glance at the (illegible) name on our badge, while a vulgar crowd stares in a bovine way. This running-the-gauntlet hardens all of us – we suffer it at weddings and at balls.

We're in! We leave our umbrella in the cloakroom, where a free fight is in happy progress, and pass to the famous lawn. Some sit on the garden seats, some stand, some lean close to the rails, some sit on the stand itself. We take a good look round – and a hearty laugh at some of the dresses, which invariably provide the comic relief, and are invariably photographed 'Seen at Ascot'. Dresses where the wearer, already purple with the heat – or is it mortification of the flesh? – has obviously gone mad dog in her wardrobe and donned

Left, watching the Grand National at Aintree, 1937

Below left, the right side of the track at Ascot: top hats and tails, 1936

Below, the wrong side: leather-lunged bookies shout the odds

Right, racing by night at Longchamps, 1934

everything so as to be on the right side. Personally, I have a great affection for these lonely figures – each of them is someone's Favourite Aunt . . . . .

When the temperature reaches a maximum, we line up to cheer the Royal Procession wheeling into the courtyard. A moment later

They appear in the Royal Box. In the Royal party we always expect to see the Portlands, the Roxburghs, the Granards, the Mar and Kellie's, the Blandfords, and popular Major Fetherstonhaugh and his wife.

We begin to rush for lunch. Even Mrs. Baldwin, who has been as immobile in her pet corner near the Judges' box as Lady Astor has been in rapid movement, follows with the crowd. Among the turbanned orientals and excited foreign guests, more famous figures appear. Lady Lavery will be there dressed dramatically, Lord d'Abernon will be cutting out any young rivals in his vicinity, Lady Furness will be particularly smart, and – most marvellous – Lord Lonsdale will be in his right clothes, conventionally dressed for once and almost self-conscious about it.

Hunger makes strange tent-fellows of us all. Some lunch in private boxes on the stands, but many more lunch in the tents. The Marlboro' is the only tent in the paddock, and the Rifle Brigade, the Cavalry, and the Bachelors' tents mean a walk across the course. These tents are enclosures within the Enclosure! The ordinary badged multitude must be content to queue outside the Luncheon Room, admiring the roses growing on the trellis and hearing the cheerful sounds from the new champagne bar.

After luncheon we walk to the Paddock to see the parades and place our bets – and the bets of our Girl Friend(s), for it is not correct form for women to bet in person at Ascot. The rest of the afternoon consists of (a) back to the stand to see the race, (b) back to the paddock, a good long stretch, (c) back to the stand, this cycle being repeated several times. The paddock is very lovely with the trees and grass and horses all lit by the flashing English sunlight familiar to admirers of Munnings. Here in the Paddock the badged fraternise with the un-badged and there is a sea of heartiness. We must not of course leave before the Royal party, the departure of which is the signal for a polite rush to the station and to the car park. Most of us are bound for London, but the local house parties return proudly to their pink villas or country-houses around Windsor where the evening closes on numbers of small dinner-dances. Those who are not completely worn out by this trial by endurance that is Ascot return on the morrow, Hunt Cup Day.

Left, the high point of Ascot: the King and Queen arrive in an open landau drawn by Windsor greys, 1934

Below, far left, 'Mr R.C. Winmill, Mrs Frederick Dickson, and Mr Winmill's zebra', 1931

Below left, Vionnet's coat of beige velvet trimmed with black ermine turns heads at the races, 1930

Right, Dufy's Ascot cover for *Vogue*, May 1935

NIGHTLIFE IN NEW YORK, LONDON, PARIS

In the thirties, smart people met to eat, talk, and entertain each other in restaurants. Café society – in the now time-honoured phrase created by *Vogue*'s Frank Crowninshield – was born. Dining out did away with stuffy rules about dressing, whom you could receive at home, orders of precedence, and interminable courses at meals. It was more fun.

In New York, the repeal of Prohibition meant the end of speak-easies, and people could talk openly about where they were spending the small hours. At El Morocco, with its zebra upholstery, silver palms, and starry ceiling, you would see, reported *Vogue*, 'the loveliest, toughest, smartest, and most celebrated women'. You went to '21' to sit at one of the red-check tables in the backroom bar and catch up with everything, or to the Spanish-style El Patio, or to the Persian Room to hear Eddy Duchin and have elbow-room to dance. Up in Harlem, you rubbed shoulders with symphony conductors and movie stars watching the 'snake-hipping' of Earl Tucker at Connie's Inn or listening to Duke Ellington at the Cotton Club, and ended the evening with an early morning snack of sausages and buckwheat cakes.

In London the smart places were still Ciro's and the Embassy, Quaglino's for superb food, and the Trocadero for the best cellars in town. Before the theatre you met at the Monseigneur bar ('theatre dinners are out') or the Ivy, beloved of stage luminaries ('Noel's corner said to be marked by a brass plate'). Afterwards, the Savoy Grill was *de rigueur* on a first night. The Marquis de Casa Maury chose the Bon Viveur in Shepherd Market for the opening party for his brilliant new Curzon cinema, which had comfortable blue armchairs and began late, so that you could join theatregoers for supper afterwards. The Blue Lantern in Ham Yard offered sheer Bohemia, while the Bat staged prize fights at dinner time every Monday, followed by dancing.

Previous page, left, Féfé's Monte Carlo nightclub in New York, 1939. WILLAUMEZ

Previous page, right, London's San Marco restaurant, designed by Oliver Messel, 1935. ERIC

Left, can-can at the Tabarin in Paris, 1936. ERIC

Above right, prize-fighting at the Bat, 1930

Right, cabaret at Harlem's Cotton Club

In Paris it was still Fouquet's for cocktails, followed by Maxim's to dine and see everyone – although the Ambassadeurs, presided over by Albert, Maxim's portly and dignified maître d'hotel, had become *'follement élégant'*, and attracted the Duke and Duchess of Windsor. But the latest in chic was the bistro. Rolls Royces lined suburban streets outside little café-restaurants with sausages hanging from the ceiling, waiting for half smart Paris to finish the best *soupe à l'oignon* in town. The Negro singers at Brick Top's, the outrageous Kiki at the Boeuf sur le Toit (now in the Hôtel Georges V) and the Grand Ecart were still the most popular cabarets: 'a tiny crowded room with a low ceiling and very little air always guarantees the success of a place in Paris'.

Opposite, above left, a snake dancer at Belle Livingstone's Country Club, New York, 1931

Opposite, above right, first night at the Curzon, 1934. After the Depression the Marquis de Casa Maury built this smart new cinema,

learned the business thoroughly, and made the venture a great success

Opposite, below left, Kiki entertains guests with outrageous songs in the Boeuf Sur le Toit in Paris, 1930

Opposite, below right, Mrs Sherman Jenney and Mrs William Wetmore photographed by resident photographer Jerome Zerbe at New York's celebrated El Morocco, 1938

Above, first night of a new film on Broadway, 1930

Above right, the Abbott Girls performing at the Ambassadeurs, Paris, 1937

Right, 'hot and sweet in Harlem'. Sketch by Vertès, 1936

PARIS PANORAMA

The Opéra has had its face washed. The great black-and-gold gates of Longchamp glisten under a new coat of gilt. The battered and rickety taxis of Paris are replaced by a fleet of spanking new cabs – painted, very aesthetically, pale green to match the tender chestnut leaves overhead, and fitted, somewhat less aesthetically, with raucous-voiced radios. Lily Pons and Yvonne Printemps and Lucienne Boyer are back home again. And so is Gertrude Stein.

Illuminated *clous* (pedestrian crossings) dot the streets at night to keep you from jay-walking. Georges Carpentier manages a new chromium-plated bar, called simply Chez Georges, into which you can scarcely wedge a foot before dinner. All the familiar Names drink tomato-juice at the new Georges Cinq Bar. American movies are the subject of passionate conversation – the new Art. Salvador Dali designs Surrealist lamps, and Jean-Michel Frank makes them and, what's more, sells them in his new shop. Bernstein's play *Espoir* chalks up its two hundred and twentieth performance to-night. *Croix de Feu* buttons replace *boutonnières* in the lapels of young men about town. The Comtesse Jean de Polignac redecorates her house with pleated red satin pilasters. And night after night, the flood-lights of Notre Dame and the Etoile and the Concorde are turned on full force – hang the expense.

The Ambassadeurs is open again – its reopening as *épatant* a show of merriment and glitter as in the Abundant Days: emeralds, ermine, champagne, Klieg lights, two orchestras, a straight-from-Hollywood dance team, and a throng of visiting Hindu potentates – caught on their way through Paris, with three hundred trunks apiece, to the London Jubilee. The native saris almost outnumbered the made-in-Paris variety.

At midnight, Victor at Florence's is baffled as to where to sandwich in another table, and pleas go up to the amiable black trumpeter to play 'Solitude' again and again. Men are all for climbing the hill to the Bal Tabarin, where dukes sit cheek by jowl with taxi-drivers,

Left, 'the Ambassadeurs is open again – as *épatant* a show of glitter and merriment as in the Abundant Days', 1935. SCHALL

where the shapeliest and most underdressed show-girls in Paris do can-cans that are can-cans, and a former burlesque vedette shinnies up a rope as she does a strip act. Cocteau's coterie follows him to his modern white Boeuf sur le Toit, dashing up-stairs between dances to hear the funny Morgan sing.

Those who want a little ribald wit mixed in the evening's pleasantry set off to hear the French Texas Guinan, known as La Môme Moineau (who wears a rhinestone bow-tie with her dinner-jacket).

Hitler is the target of all vitriol, and Mussolini the new Bosom Friend. Thanks to the recent Franco-Italo amicability, Paris has hung in the Petit Palais the cream of Italy's art treasures. The Duce's *largesse* completely astonished Paris. When Mr. Raymond Escholier went to him requesting modestly, say about a hundred canvases, the Duce replied 'What — only a hundred? We'll gladly make it three hundred,' and *sur le champ* packed up some of the greatest Giottos, Fra Angelicos, Titians, Michelangelos, Raphaels, Da Vincis, and Botticellis and shipped them off.

People have been hanging from the rafters to hear Bruno Walter's Vienna Philharmonic or Lily Pons singing *Rigoletto*, or Lucia. Bérard is doing the sets for a new Bourdet play. A new cinema, the Balzac, has added itself to the already numerous Champs-Elysées string. And Paris, getting religion, is rehearsing an ascetic Passion Play to be staged in front of Notre-Dame.

Practically every woman with a right arm is writing a book. Elizabeth de Gramont is doing her memories. Lady Mendl has published *After All*. Cécile Sorel — more memories. Mrs. Fellowes, working on one which the artist, Vertès, is illustrating. If not books, then deep interest in the feminist movement, trying to convince La Belle France that women are actually intelligent enough to vote. Or else the stage and movies. Lady Abdy making her debut on the stage in the Renaissance tragedy, *Les Cenci*. Madame de Maigret, already lost to Hollywood, signing a Metro-Goldwyn-Mayer contract.

Right, promenading in the Bois de Boulogne. Sketch by Charles Laborde, 1931

AUX QUATRE COINS DE PARIS

RITZ CAMBON

En descendant ces trois marches
l'élégante démarche
impose sa valeur.
Midi sonne et les chœurs
de chaque continent
pour un instant
se mêlent
en un seul cocktail

LE COULOIR DU RITZ

Drôle de rue, drôle de rue,
où de mémoire d'homme il n'a plu,
se disent les chiens de cette dame
en jetant leur dévolu
sur le dernier collier paru
puis soupirent à fendre l'âme

LA FOIRE AUX PUCES

Statue de la Liberté
j'offre bien mieux qu'une lumière ;
de mon état je suis crémière,
mais je quitte ma voie lactée
pour le samedi tenter l'astuce
des chercheurs à la foire aux puces

MAXIM'S

Entre les parenthèses du cuivre
qui rompent la glace des miroirs,
la mode est un conseil à suivre,
la raison est de le savoir

PARIS POEMS
by Louise de Vilmorin translated by Peter Coats Drawings by Maurice van Moppès

RITZ — CAMBON SIDE

Descending these three
   steps
In elegant procession
Can make a great
   impression
While international
   chatter passes
Among the midday
   cocktail glasses

**THE CORRIDOR OF
THE RITZ**

This is a funny street
No snow, or rain, or
   sleet
Thus say the poodles and
   the dachs
Whining for the jewelled
   collars
That cost too many
   dollars

THE FLEA MARKET

The Statue of Liberty
   only offers you a light
But I, by trade a dairy
   maid, just might,
Tempt you with a
   bargain
Next Saturday
When I stray
From my Milky Way
To the Market of Fleas
So come and see me
   please

MAXIM'S

Reflected between the
   lamps
Set in the mirrors' glint
Are fashions for you to
   follow
Good sense to take the
   hint

Women in low heels and pleated skirts looking incredibly young on the streets. Girls tossing off their hats at lunch. Debutantes appearing at parties. A surprising number of women at the Thil verses Jaks prize-fight. And always on Sunday, there is the undimmed excitement of Longchamp, after which all Paris comes back to town to sit over a Pernod at Fouquet's.

All the lavish gold plate brought out, for the first time in years, at a dinner at the English Embassy in Paris. And a spectacular dinner given at the Ambassadeurs – to raise funds for first-aid airplane transportation – with telephone connections enabling the guests to talk to simultaneous parties in four other cities – Berlin, London, Rome, and New York.

For the first time, a new airmail service within French boundaries. Two husky policewomen on the force, and new uniforms on the postmen. American red and green traffic lights on the boulevards and, already, a stirring for the Exposition of 1937 – a widening of the Pont d'Iéna and a wrecking of whole blocks of buildings to make way for the big Exposition palaces. Paris is not sitting idly twiddling its thumbs.

Above, after the races, at Fouquet's, 1934

Far left, ex-boxing champion Georges Carpentier serves from his own bar, 1935

Left, 'native saris almost outnumbered the made-in-Paris variety', 1935. The Princess Karam Kapurthala, whose saris were said to have been the inspiration for Schiaparelli's sari-coats

Below left, Lady Abdy making her stage debut in the Renaissance tragedy *Les Cenci*, 1935

Below centre, 'a Molyneux enters', 1935

Below right, Schiaparelli in her own sari-coat, 1935

NEW YORK BULLETIN

Left, luncheon at the new River Club. CECIL BEATON

Right, Prince Serge Obolensky, Mrs Harrison Williams ('the Lady Diana Cooper of New York'), and Mr Kittredge play Coney Island games at a party held on behalf of the unemployed

Far right, New York sketch by Cecil Beaton

Below right, Elsa Maxwell's party for Cole Porter at the Waldorf Astoria, 1938. Guests include Elsa Maxwell (below left, back to camera), thence clockwise: Condé Nast, Grace Moore, Frederick Lonsdale, Ethel Merman, Jules Glaenzer, Mrs Gilbert Miller

by Cecil Beaton, 1932

'This year you will find . . .' they had said, 'that most people's savings have gone pfft.' But it matters little, really. The poverty is only comparative. The hey-hey spirit prevails, and there are enough signs of festivity – the parties. Mrs. George F. Baker gave three dances during one week for her daughter, the smallest and most intimate one consisting of two hundred guests, the largest of one thousand. Mrs. Fair Vanderbilt has never been busier. And there are enough small parties, with cold turkey and champagne, to keep any boy out late any night of the week.

It is a quieter life. No one admitted three years ago that he or she might take an evening off, for fear of being out of things. But, now, some lady, leaving the tea-table, proudly boasts that she is going to spend her evening reading – straight home to bed with Mr. Proust.

This will always be remembered as the winter that produced 'Of Thee I Sing', the *Scandals*, 'Sweet and Lovely', 'Too Late', 'Time on My Hands', 'Ballyhoo', and 'Stag at Eve', Willa Cather's *Shadows on the Rock*, and Vir-

ginia Woolf's *The Waves*. There has been no dimming of lights on Broadway, no deterioration in the excellence of the drug-store food, in the riot of flora in the Goldfarb Market, in the frenzied dancing of the Lindy Hop at the Harlem Savoy. Musical celebrities arrive on every boat, and the concert halls are packed. One of the most exciting evenings I have spent was watching the Lunts playing from the wings, feeling more fiercely than ever before the glamour of the footlights, the grease-paint and pretence, knowing more definitely than before that the stage was the only life! In their rooms, Lynn and Alfred make a quick change, and make further suggestions for improvement. *Reunion in Vienna* is their current play.

I had not before been to the wrestling matches. It seems incredible that two grown-ups should mortify each other so miserably in public, that two men should suddenly don coloured tights, and proceed to bend back each other's legs and arms to inflict excruciating torments, under vivid arc-lights, to the delight of thousands.

I have only recently discovered the radio (in England, we call it the wireless) and, when I asked the German waiter to have a wireless

brought to my room, a few minutes later a surprised violinist appeared. In England, there is the choice of only two dreary programmes to tune in on, but here the radio plays all day long. You can hear Russ Columbo, Marion Harris, Jesse Crawford and his wife. There is Toscanini conducting, and Stokowski, and you can always hear 'Good-Night Sweetheart' or the address for a wonderful fur coat bargain.

I have been to the headquarters, too, and seen the possessors of these well-known voices. Even though it interferes with the microphone, Bing Crosby wears his felt hat while he sings. He has features like a Greek god caked in grease-paint, because he is rushed over from appearing personally at the Paramount Theatre. His programme is almost over, he whistles nonchalantly; his audience conjures up a vivid picture of him wending his way home down the romantic lane. In reality, he is puting on his bright chestnut-coloured overcoat and ringing for the elevator.

There is nothing skimped, simple, or economical about the new River Club. Here it is impossible to believe that we live in hard times. There is a blue mirrored ballroom, an ideal setting for lovely ladies and jewels, and

season is the new Waldorf Astoria Hotel. It is the largest hotel that has been made since the world began. The view at night from the tower building is like looking down from Babylon. Mrs. Hearst muses at the window. She chortles her well-known chortle, which she has handed down to her son. There is the already famous dining-room with the Sert frescoes, and, down-stairs, there is the delightful Savarin Restaurant, where you sit on a high stool and see many of the people who live in the hotel popping in. Cole Porter is planning, with Ray Goetz and Mr. Monty Woolley, the production of *Star Dust*. Mrs. Cole Porter has discovered a cinnamon bun on the menu. At the Waldorf, anyone may telephone for you to come up or down to his or her room. Mrs. Winston Churchill and her daughter Diana are so delighted that they talk ninety to the dozen in a clipped English accent.

This winter of depression has also seen the birth of the Whitney Museum of American Art. Mrs. Henry Payne Whitney's museum is the ideal setting for contemporary pictures.

Oh dear, oh dear, oh dearie me – even Sir Joseph Duveen has had to ask people to put the lights out after they leave a room. He just has had to economize. He has no flowers on the dining-table. And, with these times as an excuse, parties have been organised to which guests bidden must pay a contribution for being present. Mrs. Whitney lent her house to half a dozen hosts who sent facetious telegrams bidding a myriad multitude to come and pay five dollars for the unemployed. How I wish we had Mrs. Harrison Williams in England. And how I wish we could have limes with melon in England too.

an indoor terrace for lunch, with white bamboo chairs, designed to resemble a setting by Picasso. Miss Hoytie Wiborg has hung on the walls some decorative pictures by Fernand Léger, and has made a few enemies among the more conservative members of the club.

Mrs. Cobina Wright has gallantly started the Sutton Club, in a pale green room on the East River, and a new Ciro's has been launched in successful competition with the well-known haunts:— the Mansion; the place on West Fifty-Second Street; the Central Park Casino, where Eddy Duchin (than whom there is no better jazz pianist in the world) now commands his own band; and the new place on East Fifty-Eighth Street, where people sit around a huge circular bar and seem thankful for the simplicity of the modern decoration. It is the best thing Mr. Joseph Urban has ever done. Mrs. Robert McAdoo is there. She eats a gardenia for tea every day.

Certainly, the most amazing phenomenon of the present poverty-stricken, panic-stricken

PARTIES, PARTIES, PARTIES

Depression or no, there were always parties. In New York in the early Thirties, there were even parties for the unemployed – not that they were invited, but guests had to contribute five dollars, or pay exorbitantly to play Coney Island-style games. Stuffy dinners were a thing of the past. Cecil Beaton wrote that New York parties consisted of pretty women and celebrities mixed up in a 'salad' – 'the only sort of entertaining by which people are really entertained'. George Gershwin and Cole Porter were favourite guests: they would always go to the piano and make the evening one to remember.

The same international set was found at Paris parties. At one, Serge Lifar delighted the other guests by taking off his shoes, tie and dinner jacket, and jumping onto the piano, then jumping down and dancing to Germaine Taillefer's rendition of *L'Après-midi d'un Faune*.

There were dozens of fancy dress balls, including one to which everyone had to come as someone else. Cecil Beaton arrived as Elinor Glyn, while Lady Mendl disguised herself as Mistinguett. 'It is embarrassing to appear in anything elaborate,' wrote Beaton in *Vogue*. Anyone could hire from a costumiers'. The trick was to wear something unexpected and create the effect of a last minute brainwave. Elsa Maxwell, finding herself with nothing to wear to Leon Bailby's pink party, arrived wrapped in a pink satin bedspread from her room at the Ritz.

As well as fancy dress, there was a craze for nursery games – like musical chairs, blindman's buff, sticking the pig, and bobbing for apples – although the latter went out of favour very quickly as none of the women would risk losing their new eyelashes. One of the best mystery parties was 'Who is the Lady in the Trunk?' Footmen carried in a trunk which, guests were told, contained a lady they had all seen in public, an artist. The trunk was opened, and a woman, disguised in a white satin dress, a mask, scarf, gloves, and high boots, stepped out. Only Mrs. Michael Arlen guessed correctly: it was the French actress Gaby Morlay.

Unquestionably, the most brilliant parties were given by Elsa Maxwell – with other people's money. People paid her between sixteen and sixty thousand dollars to make

their parties sparkle. Once she gave a Hallowe'en party at the Waldorf Astoria, at which gentlemen in tailcoats were found peering under beds for pumpkins throughout the whole labyrinth of the hotel. On another occasion she converted the Waldorf roof into a farmyard. Cows soared up in the elevators along with 400 guests dressed as yokels and scarecrows and their more tractable livestock, including two donkeys, twelve hogs, and a lamb. Prince Serge Obolensky brought a pig, and Mrs. Henry Luce was accompanied by a duck. Champagne fizzed from a mechanical Moët cow, and the hotel staff got to sit on the plush and gold chairs in the servants' quarters, as their wooden ones had been commandeered for the event.

Perhaps best known was Miss Maxwell's scavenger hunt, for which guests had to comb Paris for a list of oddly assorted items that included a slipper worn by Mistinguett that night.

Mistinguett's poor maid didn't stand a chance against the society scavengers and had to face the brunt of the star's anger when she

Above, 'statues' at the Comtesse Pecci-Blunt's Bal Blanc, including Boris Kochno and Christian Bérard, 1930

Left, Cole Porter, always the life of the party, entertaining guests with one of his songs, 1934

Below, a *fête champêtre* organized by Elsa Maxwell at the Baron de Gunzbourg's house in the Bois. Guests in the cart include Mr and Mrs Cole Porter, 1931

Left, Mme Henry Bernstein and Mme Misia Sert, striking and mysterious figures in black and white representing Night and Day at André Durst's 'Inhabitants of the Forest' Ball in Paris, 1938

Right, Mr and Mrs Douglas Fairbanks flanking Constance Bennett at Elsa Maxwell's Waldorf Astoria barn dance, 1937

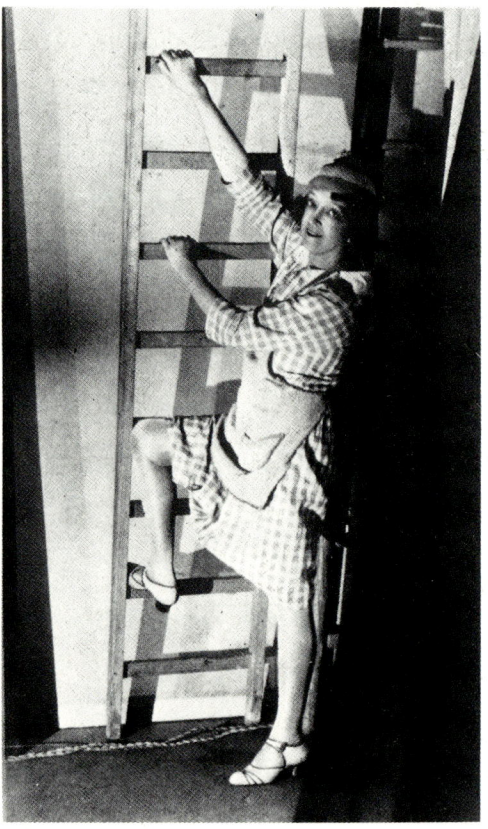

ELSA MAXWELL'S SCAVENGER LIST
One red bicycle lamp
One cooked sausage
One live animal other than a dog
One swan from the Bois
One slipper worn by Mistinguett that night
One handkerchief belonging to the Baron Maurice de Rothschild
One hat from Mrs. Reginald Fellowes
One live duchess
One autographed photograph of royalty signed that night
One red stocking
One mauve comb
Three red hairs
One pompon from a sailor's hat
The cleverest man in Paris

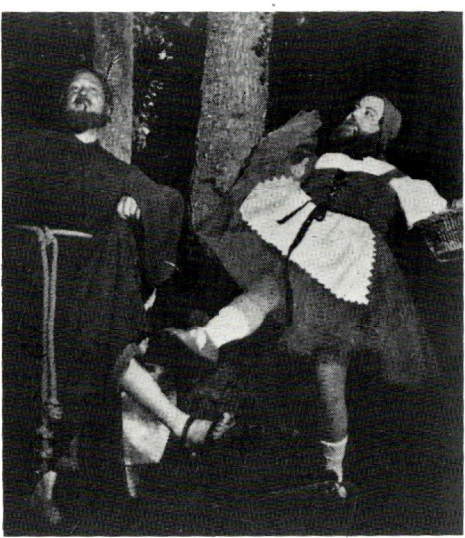

Above, Elsa Maxwell impersonating Aristide Briant at her birthday party, held in the Paris house of the Hon Daisy Fellowes, 1930.
HOYNINGEN-HUENE

Above right and right, fellow guests Cecil Beaton as Elinor Glyn and Lady Mendl as Mistinguett

Left, two more guests at André Durst's Forest Ball: Carl Erickson as a hermit, and Christian Bérard as Red Riding Hood. Both were *Vogue* illustrators

Opposite, guests watch the circus at Lady Mendl's famous party at Versailles, 1938

returned to her dressing room to find all her shoes gone. However they were all returned the next day, tied to massive flowering plants and bunches of orchids, to make amends.

Elsa Maxwell gave her own rules for party-giving in *Vogue*. First, ruthlessness; second, a hostess cannot have an established 'position' i.e. in finance, religion, or diplomacy. No snobs or dull people. Do not let guests do what they want – no guests want to do what they want. Use one room only, which should always be too small for the number of guests. Light it brilliantly. One should enter a party to sounds of some kind. 'I once gave a party in a room too cold and cavernous, so I hastily procured some beehives, and successfully concealed them in the room, so that the ears of the guests were assailed by a pleasant buzzing during lulls in the music.' Never show the slightest anxiety. Always endeavour to incur the opposition of one or two of the 'social powers-that-be', so that feelings will run high, and people will take sides and either go to the party or stay away. Finally, a new idea, plus a sense of humour, makes a party.

Another party that remained on people's lips for years was Elsie Mendl's Circus Ball. Lady Mendl, who sometimes wore emerald stars in her hair to emphasise its blue tint, prepared for the event for 10 months. Clever lighting turned night into day in the garden of the Villa Trianon, her Versailles home. Constance Spry provided three plane-loads of flowers from London. There were three orchestras – Negro, Cuban, and an all-women Hungarian waltz band – and a specially built dance pavilion with a dance floor inlaid with millions of tiny springs that made guests feel as if they were floating – or as if they had had too much champagne. An elegant circus of satin-clad acrobats and white ponies imported from Finland provided on-going entertainment. Lady Mendl spent the afternoon being coached to be the pony master. Everything went without a hitch until one of the ponies jumped the ring and hid in the rosebushes. Before the night was over, all the women decided they wanted a pony for a pet.

Left, the Georgian Group ball at Lord and Lady Jersey's Adam house Osterley Park – or rather, a full-dress repeat performance staged especially for *Vogue* to photograph, 1939. Stage designer Oliver Messel organized the ball and designed the costumes

Left, the Prince and Princess Karam de Kapurthala in sumptuous costumes as the Duke and Duchess of Lorraine, 1939. HORST

Above, the buffet at the Osterley ball. On the left is Oliver Messel, who played a violin during the ball

Below, more Osterley guests: Mrs Somerset Maugham, Mark Ogilvie Grant, and Lord Rosse

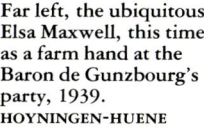

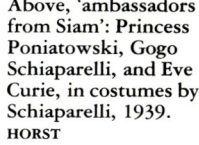

Far left, the ubiquitous Elsa Maxwell, this time as a farm hand at the Baron de Gunzbourg's party, 1939.
HOYNINGEN-HUENE

Above, 'ambassadors from Siam': Princess Poniatowski, Gogo Schiaparelli, and Eve Curie, in costumes by Schiaparelli, 1939.
HORST

IN THE GROOVE

'Swing is the musical fashion of the hour. Not to know the work of such swing artists as Thomas 'Fats' Waller and Jack 'Big Gate' Teagarden (gate meaning the ability to swing) is to confess such a dowdiness as would have been shown some years ago by someone who supposed the rumba to be one of the larger vertebrae. Judging by the heavy white-tie and Schiaparelli attendance at such New York swing saloons as the Onyx Club, swing music has penetrated the ritziest circles. It is even robust enough to appeal to Ernest Hemingway.' Thus wrote Wilder Hobson in *Vogue* in 1936. Hard to define, swing had elements of 'hot' jazz music, the 'sweet' sounds of crooners like Bing Crosby and Rudy Vallee, and the big band sound of Guy Lombardo and Glenn Miller. Swing men ('cats') who played it on their clarinets, trumpets, and drums took off, abandoning lines and dots and improvising variations on a theme and creating new melodies. They described its effect as 'it sends me'. Indeed, no statement was more enlightening than Duke Ellington's 'It don't mean a thing if it ain't got that swing'. Benny Goodman, Tommy Dorsey, Louis Armstrong, and Count Basie played the real stuff.

Although you listened to swing as much as danced to it, America was swept by a dance craze called the Big Apple (a Negro expression for bottom). This involved a mixture of shuffling, stomping, and rump-rotating steps such as 'Kickin' the Mule', and 'Peelin' the Apple'. It was followed by the acrobatic jitterbug. Neither dance really took off in England. Lesley Blanch, writing in *Vogue*, had to admit that, no matter what Irving Berlin's song said about everybody having rhythm, the English did not.

Left, Eddy Duchin, 'who plays the piano like a bored, irresistible rag doll', 1936

Insets: Pee Wee Irwin, trumpeting in water and playing finger cymbals, 1939

Bottom row, left to right: 'Leslie Hutchinson and Reggie Service, riding high', 1939; Charles MacArthur tootling on his silver clarinet, 1939; blues singer Maxine Sullivan at the Onyx Club, New York, 1938; and Jack (Big Gate) Teagarden, who played trombone for Paul Whiteman for many years, 1936

Right, 'fruity dark voices Harlemise Gilbert, while Bill Robinson taps intoxicatingly to Sullivan's hotcha-ed rhythms in the riotous *Hot Mikado*', 1939

Music notes

'Music is "smart" in England,' wrote *Vogue* in 1932. 'Lady Cunard sings the whole of the Ring through at the back of her box.' An indefatigable supporter of her friend Sir Thomas Beecham, Emerald Cunard deserved much of the credit for filling the boxes at Covent Garden with society. You might also see 'three hundred ladies determinedly listening to music' in her Marie Laurencin drawing-room, lent for one of the fashionable Aeolus concerts organised by Miss Olga Lynn. As the decade wore on, and events worsened in Germany and Austria, London did become in a sense the musical centre of the world. Many musicians, including Toscanini – 'as incorruptible an idealist as musician' – and the singer Lotte Lehmann left their homelands, and Bruno Walter became a French citizen.

Nonetheless, the composer Constant Lambert subtitled his book, *Music Ho* (1934), 'A study of music in decline' and lamented the lack of revolutionary musical ideas since Stravinsky. He could not have foreseen that four years later the American John Cage would write *Construction I,* which used piano strings played with felt-headed sticks. British composers of the decade included Vaughan Williams, Arnold Box, Benjamin Britten, just in his twenties, and William Walton, whose *Belshazzar's Feast* incorporated jazz rhythms, and whose symphony was performed in 1934 without the final movement, because he could not finish it in time. There was also the eccentric Lord Berners, who kept a canary-yellow 1900 automobile in his drive as a gazebo. Pink-and-blue-dyed doves fluttered about his house, and a white horse was said to wander into his drawing room for a cup of tea.

1934 saw the birth of Glyndebourne – 'roulades and cadenzas among the buttercups and moo-cows of the Sussex countryside'. John Christie, a former Eton science master who had married the Mozartian singer Audrey Mildmay, built an opera house next to his country house and proceeded to stage professional performances and serve dinners in the newly constructed restaurants at 5/- or 10/- a meal. Pioneers of rural opera enjoyed chugging out of Victoria in full evening dress at midday. Toscanini – notoriously difficult to please – visited and vowed it better than Salzburg.

In America also, serious music was received

enthusiastically. In 1937 Toscanini conducted 10 concerts with the New York Philharmonic on NBC to an audience of millions and a studio audience of 1,000, who were given satin programmes that were guaranteed not to crackle. You could also hear the Metropolitan Opera on the radio on Saturday afternoons and the Detroit Symphony and the New York Philharmonic on Sundays: altogether a total of 10,250,000 families listened in each week.

Live concerts also thrived. In 1937 Koussevitzsky founded the Berkshire Festival at Tanglewood, Massachusetts, and by 1939 there were 279 symphony orchestras across the country. Opera also flourished; singers who drew the crowds at the New York Metropolitan Opera House included Lotte Lehmann, the Hungarian Rosa Pauly as Elektra, Kirsten Flagstad as Isolde (her Tristan was the 110 kg [240 lb] Laurenz Melchior), and the pretty French coloratura soprano Lily Pons, who made her American debut in 1931. The best marketed of all was Grace Moore, 'the extraordinary Tennessee triller', who by 1935 could call herself the greatest cinema-opera star in the world. She sang before Edward VIII and her Covent Garden concert in 1935 was a sellout at £5 a ticket.

Left, a cross-section of the Metropolitan Opera House during *Tristan and Isolde*, drawn by Alajálov, 1937. Far left, top, sweethearts in the corridor. Just below, ushers chew on cold hot dogs, fearful of the eye of their captain. Below, people run for their boxes; they will breathe heavily for fifteen minutes, in time to Wagner.
Just in front of the first row orchestra, the prompter, with his book before him. Next to him, a guard. Across the page, in the basement, the musicians' dressing room, with two musicians playing two-handed bridge. On the other side of the steps, the male chorus. Above them, a live horse actor. Next door, with a guard outside, the star's dressing room, which after the final curtain will be filled with family and friends. Above, the female chorus dressing room. Across the hall, the seamstresses sew day and night.
Just above, the stagehands are busy with the dice. The elevator holds a Scandinavian King. On the same floor, the wardrobe room, with gowns brilliant with rhinestones. And again, love in the passageway. Most of the floor above is devoted to storage rooms, in blackness. In one room next door, in the brightness of bulbs burning unshaded, the wigmakers fuss with the blonde plaits of Brünnehilde and Sieglinde. The top floor is a dancing mass of ballet. No-one in the whole house ever listens to Tristan and Isolde, ever peeks out to see what has brought the audience to the pageant

BALLETOMANIA

Left, 'The First Crime', a dramatic moment in the Monte Carlo Ballet Russe's interpretation of Beethoven's Seventh Symphony, 1939. ANTON BRUEHL

Above, Baranova pirouetting against a Dufy drop in *Beach*, 1934

Above right, Toumanova and Jasinsky dancing in *Mozartiana*, with Mozart music and costumes by Bérard, 1933

Diaghilev died on the Lido in Venice in 1929, but ballet survived the disintegration of his Ballets Russes to become the most popular of the arts during the Thirties. 'Opera season is all jewels and tiaras,' wrote *Vogue*. 'But the Royal Box and Lady Cunard's box give way when the ballet comes to picturesque smoking bohemians. This is the most thrilling audience that Covent Garden knows – because it is the most enthusiastic.'

Balletomanes, 'tense with culture', also crowded into the Ballet Club on Ladbroke Road run by the impassioned Marie Rambert ('she works like a fury, speaks five languages, and is a Slav'), or went to the Camargo Ballet, founded by Lopokova, Ninette de Valois, and Anton Dolin, who produced the ballet *Façade* – 'charming and delicious nonsense' – with music by William Walton and choreography by Frederick Ashton. Audiences also made the trip up Rosebery Avenue to Sadler's Wells, newly opened in 1931, where Lilian Baylis of the Old Vic and Ninette de Valois founded the Vic-Wells Ballet. Its taste, freshness, and ingenuity were quickly recognized. 'In a shower of streamers, in a hullaballoo of gallery yells, Lillian Baylis, with a red and white bouquet, tells of her five-year plan for British ballet,' wrote *Vogue* of a performance there. 'A strange assortment of presents are brought on during her speech. Boxes, pots of flowers, bicycle tyres are laid at the feet of favourite dancers.'

The Vic-Wells prima ballerina was the adored young Alicia Markova, 'as classical as Mozart and as vertebrate in her liveliness as Scarlatti.' In 1939, another Vic-Wells dancer, the sixteen-year-old Margot Fonteyn – otherwise known as Peggy Hookham – was 'dazzling with her incredible technique' in Stravinsky's *Baiser de la Fée*. 'She will become one of the greatest stars of our day,' predicted *Vogue*.

In 1933 Georges Balanchine was lured across the Atlantic to set up the American School of Ballet. In Monte Carlo, Colonel de Basil resuscitated the fragments of the Ballets Russes, with Massine as choreographer and many old hands from the Diaghilev days, and made his company a huge popular and financial success. By 1938 a vast number of major dancers and artists had merged into a massive ballet syndicate calling itself United Art Incorporated, based in Monte Carlo. Massine and Fokine, Ashton and Nijinska, Lichine and Lifar, Matisse, Dali, and Bérard were among its members. Dali made a stir in its production of the Venusberg ballet by crowning Lohengrin's helmet with surrealist swans' necks ending in hands, with the corps de ballet all crutches, kidneys, and chic gowns executed by Chanel, topped with huge fish-heads.

Above, two masks by Dérain for the ballet *Fastes*, 1933

Above right, Leonide Massine and Tatiana Riabouchinska in *Scuola di Ballo*, 1933.
HOYNINGEN-HUENE

Right, Dérain putting the finishing touches to his decor for the ballet *La Concurrence*, presented by the Monte Carlo Ballets Russes, with music by Auric and choreography by Balanchine, 1932

Above, a scene from *Foyer de Danse*, staged at Marie Rambert's Ballet Club. The ballet, composed by Frederick Ashton, was inspired by Degas' studies of dancers, and was performed to music by Lord Berners, 1932

Left, Tamara Toumanova and Leon Woizikovsky in Kochno's *Cotillon* in Paris, 1932

Above, Margot Fonteyn, prima ballerina with the Vic-Wells Ballet, 1939.
GILBERT ADAMS

Right, Marie Rambert, inspired teacher and founder of the Ballet Rambert, 1936

Top margin, sketches by Dérain for *La Concurrence*, 1932

Clenched fists and bare feet

'The tense business of modern dancing is a cultural phenomenon that no-one, even those intimately connected with it, seems able to explain very well,' wrote E. J. Kahn, Jr, in *Vogue*, 1938. In Germany its chief exponent was Mary Wigman; in the United States, Doris Humphrey, Charles Weidman, and Martha Graham – 'a lithe, sexless figure with long straight hair, and a face set into an expressionless mask'. Stark, intellectual, and harshly dramatic, modern dance used music merely as a frame for dance, and infuriated more audiences than it pleased. *Vogue*'s Marya Mannes considered it 'artistically a blasphemy. Mary Wigman's violent angular labours, her squattings and piston-arms and stampings and twistings leave us as cold as does a Duchamp abstraction. If there is beauty in that agonized art, that desperate translation of the brain into the body, then we are wholly without vision.'

Left, frieze from the American Ballet's *Errante*, in which a woman, symbolically weighted by a stage-long satin train, tries to flee from the spectres of her fears and passions. The ballet was designed by Tchelitchew and directed by Balanchine, 1936. NELSSON

Below, Covarrubias' view of 'the unhappy moderns', 1936

Above left, the German Mary Wigman, one of the founders of modern dance, 1930

Top, blonde Hanya Holm. She concentrated on the three-dimensional quality of dance, 1938

Above, Doris Humphrey and Charles Weidman in *Duo Drama*. 'The rhythm of Humphrey's dancing is derived from the alternation between unbalance and recovery and the audience is most excited when recovery comes just in time to save unbalance from turning into disaster', 1938

Left, Martha Graham giving a dance recital, 1933

RAZZMATAZZ

In England, Noel Coward, C.B. Cochran, and Ivor Novello kept up the British tradition of musical revues. Cochran's *Streamline* starred Tilly Losch and Nijinsky's daughter Kyra and was designed by Oliver Messel and Cecil Beaton; *Vogue* pronounced it a 'crashing success'. Acknowledged star of British cabaret was the risqué Douglas Byng, while Gracie Fields and George Formby Jr. were the big names in the otherwise dying music hall. Musicals with a Tyrolean theme were popular, including Franz Léhar's operetta *The Land of Smiles*. And a 'wonderfully vulgar' musical comedy called *Me and My Gal* set the whole world dancing the Lambeth Walk.

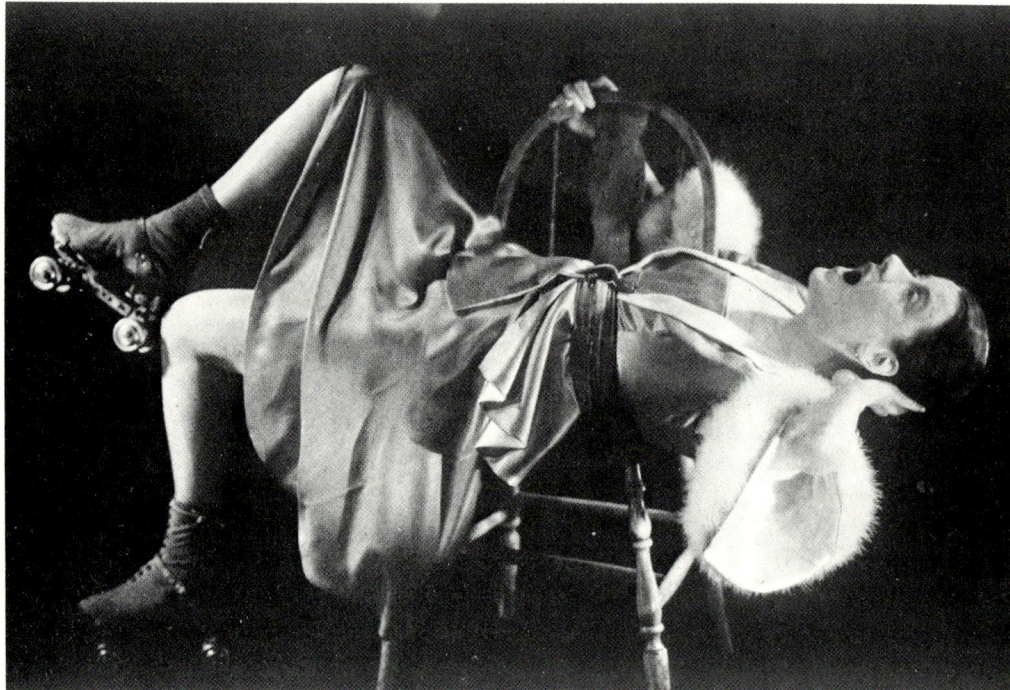

Above left, a scene from *Bow Bells*, starring Harriet Hoctor, at the Hippodrome, 1932

Left, Bea Lillie doing a skating act, 1931.
STEICHEN

Above, the cockney Jessie Matthews in one of her costumes for *Hold My Hand*, 1932

Right, four moods of the come-hither Brazilian singer Carmen Miranda, star of the revue *The Streets of Paris*, 1939. 'She sings huskily with the effect of an electric light bulb crashing'

Far right, 'rhythm and balance': the Negro dancer Josephine Baker, 1930

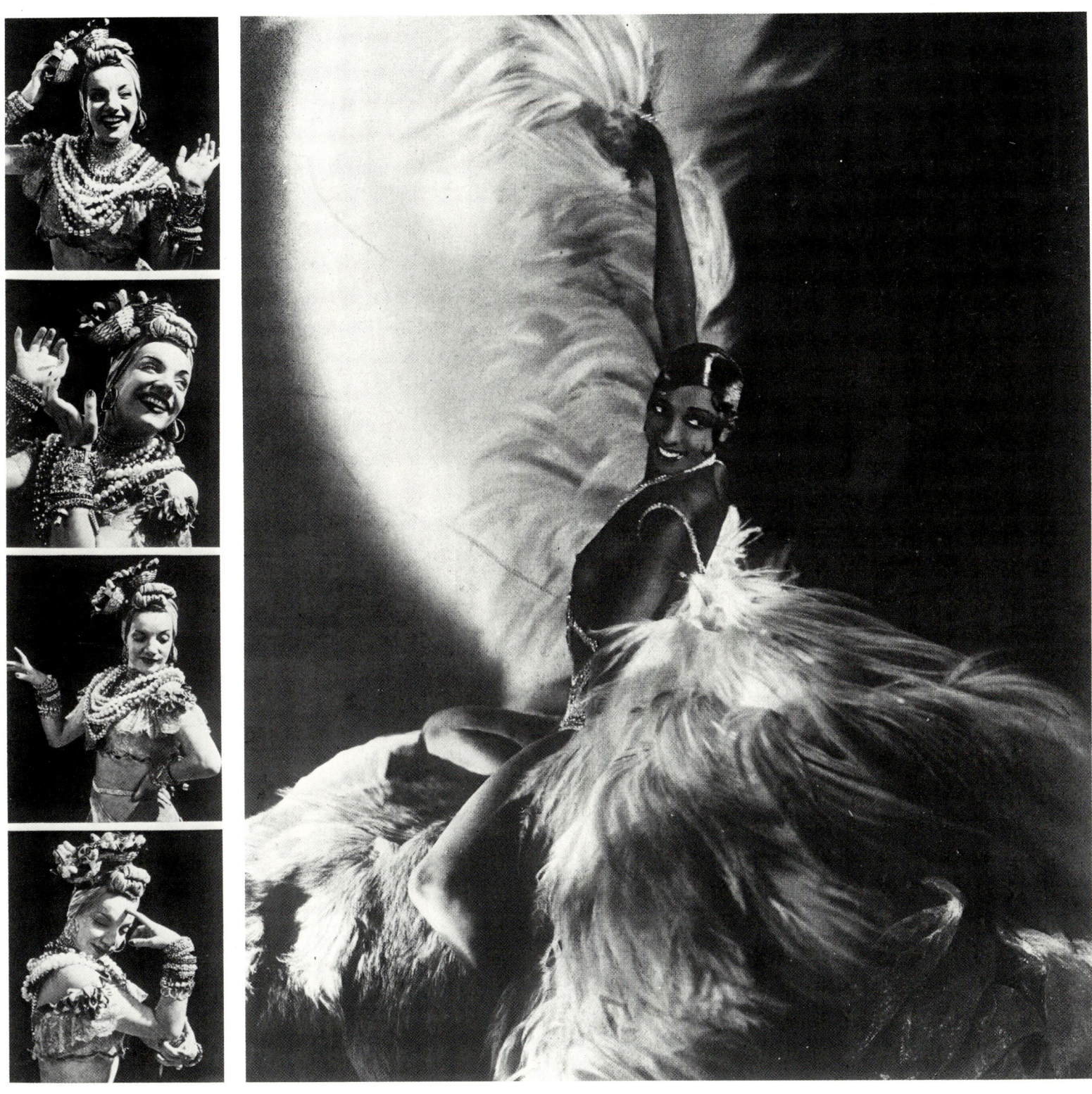

Musical shows, wrote *Vogue* in 1934, depended on 'good music, good gags, good-lookers, and Pace' – a recipe admirably fulfilled by the American shows of Rodgers and Hart, Irving Berlin, George Gershwin, Cole Porter, and Jerome Kern. They gave you syrupy songs, intoxicating orchestration, and *de rigueur* tap dance routines, and usually went on to become blockbuster films. Fred Astaire and Ginger Rogers, dancing with effortless disciplined grace in such films as *Top Hat*, *Shall We Dance*, and *Flying Down to Rio*, have become a symbol of the Thirties.

Sequence above and right, the inimitable Fred Astaire, in a sequence from *The Castles*, about the dancing couple Irene and Vernon Castle, 1939

Left, Fred Astaire and Claire Luce, stars of *Gay Divorce*, in an off-stage moment, 1933. Luce was an early successor to Astaire's sister Adele after she left the brother-and-sister team for marriage to Lord Charles Cavendish. STEICHEN

Fred Astaire

Right and above right, 'rhythm in chiffon', Ginger Rogers, 1937. She was, wrote *Vogue*, 'a girl who, though her features are far from fatal, has the world at her feet, top of the films' popularity poll'

Sequence left, another dancing couple: the De Marcos, who charmed audiences at the Grosvenor House, 1935. 'Dark as the mane of a blue-black Arab; fleet as the wind in his mane; proud as the arch of his neck; perfect and delicate as the stance of his hoofs; all these are the De Marcos, dancing.' STEICHEN

SEEN ON THE STAGE

The Thirties watched Noel Coward moving from triumph to triumph. 1930 saw him and his favourite leading lady Gertie Lawrence regaling audiences in *Private Lives*. 'A preposterous trifle,' sniffed *Vogue*, nonetheless reluctantly admiring. 'It is cocktails, cocktails all the way. He has great gifts. It is a pity they do not mature.' But those who thought Coward incapable of anything serious had to eat their words at *Cavalcade* (1931). The entire royal family attended one performance of this true-blue, 22-scene panorama of England from the Zulu Wars up to the present – a cheering fillip during Depression days. One scene showed a crowd of 400 swaying to and fro in delirious rejoicing on Armistice Day, with even the boxes nearest the stage filled with actors in turn-of-the-century costume. Audiences were reduced to hysterical sobbing, and after the first night Coward is reported to have said, 'After all, it is a pretty exciting thing these days to be English'. '*Cavalcade* has elevated Coward into a sort of national possession,' wrote *Vogue*. Further successes followed – the somewhat bitter *Words and Music*, with the immortal song 'Mad Dogs and Englishmen', *Conversation Piece*, *Design for Living*, *Tonight at 8.30* (nine one-act plays put on in threes), and *Operette* – and Coward became confident enough to issue an ultimatum to first-nighters to get to the theatre on time or risk receiving seats well in the rear – 'a fate almost too gruesome to contemplate'.

'Do you follow Laurence Olivier's career as an actor?' wrote *Vogue* in 1935. 'You should, for he is now one of the three best actors on the English stage.' That year Olivier, 'looking like a portrait of a young man by Bronzino, with built-out bridge to his nose', played a moving Romeo, with John Gielgud taking the part of Mercutio. The two swapped roles half-way through the run, but were nearly upstaged by Edith Evans as the Nurse, while Peggy Ashcroft's Juliet was 'a thing of pristine beauty'. Gielgud also made a brilliant Hamlet. 'He is destined to be the Henry Irving of 1940,' predicted *Vogue*, noting that children were going to see the play in the holidays instead of *Peter Pan*.

Everyone's darlings of the theatre were the husband and wife team Alfred Lunt and Lynn Fontanne, 'the best combination since the

Left, 'the modern mask' of Katharine Hepburn, by Cecil Beaton, 1935. Hepburn began her acting career on the stage and alternated between New York and Hollywood throughout the decade. *Vogue* wrote: 'Hepburn has the lean thighs and broad bladelike shoulders of a mythical huntress . . . she is a copper wire strung to uttermost tension: her voice is the twanging of that wire.'

Right, Tallulah Bankhead, looking like a picture by Sargent, in the part of her career: Regina Giddens in Lillian Hellman's *The Little Foxes*, 1939. HORST

Guitrys'. Cecil Beaton found them 'totally delightful' as the lovers in Robert Sherwood's *Reunion in Vienna*. They acted with Coward in his *Design For Living*, and played Jupiter and Alcmena in the London performance of *Amphytrion 38*, a Theban bedroom prank by Jean Giraudoux, France's leading playwright. In the French production their parts were taken by Madeleine Ozeray and Louis Jouvet, France's greatest actor, who took the leads in most of Giraudoux' plays, including *Ondine* and the anti-war drama *The Trojan War will not take Place* (1935).

Other plays with a particularly Thirties' flavour included *French Without Tears* by Terence Rattigan, with Penelope Dudley Ward,

and Ben Travers' farces at the Aldwych. Author-director J. B. Priestley turned out almost a play a year, family plays like *Dangerous Corner*, *Eden End* (with Ralph Richardson in the lead), and *Time and the Conways*, which played very effectively with the theories of time developed by J. W. Dunne. W. H. Auden, Louis MacNiece, Stephen Spender, and Christopher Isherwood wrote left-wing plays for select audiences. *Love On the Dole* with Wendy Hiller portrayed the working-class drama of a mill girl forced to become a bookie's mistress in order to support her unemployed family. It ran for nearly 400 performances.

T. S. Eliot had a significant success with *Murder in the Cathedral* at the Mercury Theatre:

Far left, Charles Laughton, versatile character-actor both on the stage and in films, 1933. He was perhaps best known for his movies, *The Private Life of Henry VIII* and *Mutiny on the Bounty*. He was married to Elsa Lanchester. BRUEHL

Above, Noel Coward and Gertrude Lawrence in the 'preposterously sophisticated trifle', *Private Lives*, 1931. In New York, the parts of Victor and Sybil were taken by Laurence Olivier and his wife Jill Esmond

Left, Flora Robson, 1933. She played opposite Charles Laughton in *Measure for Measure*. HORST

Vogue called it 'by far the best writing in years'. But the American giant of the theatre, Eugene O'Neill, made audiences sag with exhaustion at more than six hours of melodramatic emotion in *Mourning Becomes Electra* at the New York Theater Guild. 'Too gangrenous a theme,' was the verdict of *Vogue*'s Lesley Blanch. Pirandello's *As You Desire Me* was pronounced vague and baffling, and *Too True to be Good* by the septuagenarian *enfant terrible* of the English theatre Bernard Shaw turned out to be a reworking of many of his old themes. Even Bea Lillie's vaudeville tricks could not save it from seeming weak and strained. In Paris, Jean Cocteau treated audiences to several audacious works including *Les Parents Terribles*, the story of a son with a too-loving mother who falls in love with his father's mistress, and *La Machine Infernale*, a reworking of the Oedipus myth.

Left, a scene from *Cavalcade*, Noel Coward's patriotic entertainment at Drury Lane, with Binnie Barnes as the cabaret singer on the stage upon the stage, 1931. Six hydraulic lifts raised the cast of 400 on to the stage. *Vogue*'s reporter wrote: 'Coming late into the darkened theatre, I was thrust into a world of 1900. The tiers of boxes flanking the stage were filled with people dressed in the fashions of that time . . . One of the actors stepped out in front of the curtain and announced the thrilling news that Mafeking had been relieved . . . The noise of cheering that followed was deafening . . . The next scene revealed not the stage, but the audience – a theatre of 1900 going mad over a Boer war victory; the people jumping from box to box, embracing one another; the women throwing fans into the air . . . The enthusiasm was infectious, and the whole theatre – our part of the theatre, too – went mad, some people bursting into hysterical sobbing'

But what people flocked to see were lavish musical spectaculars, preferably with as many revolving stages as possible. *Autumn Crocus* and *White Horse Inn* headed a list of many with a Tyrolean theme. 'We have never been so tyrolised over before,' wrote one critic. Other long runs included *The Barretts of Wimpole Street*, with America's first lady of the stage, Katharine Cornell, taking the part of Elizabeth in the New York production, and *Grand Hotel*, with its motion-picture scenes and flashes. Tallulah Bankhead, looking like a picture by Sargent, finally found a part worthy of her and her husky, weary, glamour-laden voice as the hard-as-nails Regina in Lillian Hellman's *Little Foxes*, 'a play as smarting as a short smash to the jaw'. The young Welshman Emlyn Williams strutted the boards in his own thriller *Night Must Fall*, and played opposite Sybil Thorndike in *The Corn Is Green*,

his tribute to the schoolmistress who had encouraged him to go to Oxford.

Two imports thrilled American audiences: Raymond Massey, with a voice like balm, played the reluctant president in Robert Sherwood's play *Abe Lincoln in Illinois*, and Robert Morley as the eponymous hero in *Oscar Wilde* presented his case from the witness box with dignity and tact, 'swaying his great bulk rhythmically'. Lord Alfred Douglas wrote expressing his pleasure at the play.

This and many other plays tangled with England's overzealous censor during the Thirties. *Victoria Regina* by Laurence Housman opened in America with Helen Hayes some time before Gilbert Miller's London production, with Rex Whistler's wittily exaggerated sets, was allowed to go ahead – although it was hard to see what the fuss was about, unless it was John

Brown telling the monarch to 'poot yer hat straight'. 'A crowned sugar-bowl,' one critic called the play. The mood was sentimental and affectionate, and women sobbed throughout.

Clare Boothe Luce's *The Women*, which purported to unveil the true nature of women, was a different story. This milestone play, performed by a cast of 40 actresses including Ilka Chase, opened in New York in December 1936 and made a million dollars in its first year. Mrs. Roosevelt proclaimed her pity that anyone had to know creatures of such depravity, and the author was called a vicious and cynical harpy, a slut with a poison pen. The play toured America, opened simultaneously in many countries, and even Hitler was said to want it, if only the author would give proof of Aryanism. Explicit political satire was proscribed in England, for fear of aggravating the

Top, Laurence Olivier as Romeo, and above, John Gielgud as Mercutio, 1935. Above right, another 1935 production of *Romeo and Juliet*, with Katharine Cornell and Basil Rathbone

delicate situation in Europe. However many plays echoed the concerns of the age. In New York Orson Welles and John Houseman staged *Julius Caesar* as a modern propaganda play about fascism, with Welles as Brutus. In its discussion of a forthcoming war, Robert Sherwood's *Idiot's Delight* was interpreted as defeatist on one side and hailed by the Peace Pledge Union on the other. 'You can refuse to fight!' urges one of the characters. The play opened in London in March 1938, just ten days after Hitler invaded Austria.

Top left, Alfred Lunt and Lynn Fontanne in Giraudoux' 'Theban bedroom prank', *Amphitryon 38*, at the Theatre Guild, 1937

Above, Orson Welles in a sack suit as Brutus, in his own production (with John Houseman) of *Julius Caesar*, 1938. Performed on a startlingly bare stage, with Caesar in a dark

green uniform 'much like the costuming of any modern dictator', the play, wrote *Vogue*, 'now has the movement and colour of a modern propaganda play on Fascism'

Top right, a scene from Laurence Housman's *Victoria Regina*, with Helen Hayes as the ageing Victoria receiving Disraeli in the tartan tent

at Balmoral. The sets were designed by Rex Whistler, 1936

Centre right, a violent scene from Clare Boothe Luce's controversial comedy *The Women*, in which an all-female cast presented 'an authentic uncensored report on the complex business of being a woman', 1937

Above, Robert Morley as Oscar Wilde in the play of the same name, 1938

Right, a dignified Raymond Massey as the President in *Abe Lincoln in Illinois*, 1939

Top, four moods of Elisabeth Bergner, 1937. She was one of Germany's finest actresses before being expelled by the Nazis for being Jewish

Above, Rex Harrison, Diana Wynyard, and Anton Walbrook in Noel Coward's *Design for Living*, 1939. Once deemed 'too ambisextrous' for London, the play was earlier staged in New York with Coward and the Lunts in the leading roles. Coward himself played the playwright Leo, reading the reviews for his latest play: 'Thin. The characterization falters, but the dialogue is polished, nay brilliant.' He delighted in beating the critics to it

Right, Ralph Richardson, star of the stage version of *The Citadel*, 1939

Above right, Ruth Gordon, Raymond Massey, and Pauline Lord as the tragic triangle in *Ethan Frome*, 1936

Right, the eternal triangle with incest thrown in: Jean Marais and Germaine Dermoz as the son and his over-loving mother in Jean Cocteau's *Parents Terribles*, 1938

A LONDON FIRST NIGHT, 1936

1.	Claire Luce	33.	Mrs Cochran
2.	Dodie Smith	34.	Ian Hay
3.	Jack Wilson	35.	Lady Castlerosse
4.	Godfrey Winn	36.	C.B. Cochran
5.	Marie Tempest	37.	Lady Queensberry
6.	Sir Edward Marsh	38.	Anita Elson
7.	Elisabeth Bergner	39.	Dorothy Dickson
8.	Lady Bridget Poulett	40.	Mrs Ormond Lawson Johnston
9.	Charles Birkin	41.	Edward Knoblock
10.	Mrs Charles Sweeny	42.	Ormond Lawson Johnston
11.	Charles Sweeny	43.	Raymond Massey
12.	Mrs Claude Leigh	44.	Marchioness of Milford Haven
13.	Gordon Selfridge	45.	H.R.H. The Duchess of Kent
14.	Lady Kemball-Cook	46.	The Marquis of Milford Haven
15.	Frank Lawton	47.	H.R.H. The Duke of Kent
16.	Lord Headfort	48.	Gladys Calthrop
17.	Lady Headfort	49.	Frances Day
18.	Lady Oxford	50.	Noel Coward
19.	Mrs Gilbert Miller	51.	Lord Londonderry
20.	Gilbert Miller	52.	Lady Londonderry
21.	Beverley Nichols	53.	Anthony Eden
22.	Lord Willingdon	54.	Lady Mairi Stenart
23.	Lady Carisbrooke	55.	Countess Haugwitz-Reventlow
24.	Mrs Anthony Eden		
25.	H.G. Wells	56.	Lady Plunket
26.	Sir Victor Warrender	57.	Lady Juliet Duff
27.	Lady Warrender	58.	Ivor Novello
28.	The Marquis de Casa Maury	59.	Lady Diana Duff-Cooper
29.	The Marquise de Casa Maury	60.	Lady Cunard
30.	Vincent Paravicini	61.	Rex Whistler
31.	Mrs Paravicini		
32.	Evelyn Laye		

BOOKS IN VOGUE

LOOK HOMEWARD ANGEL
by Thomas Wolfe, 1930

This appears to be less a book than a torrent of impassioned prose telling everything about the life of a boy growing into young manhood, his family – including a patient, hard-working, avaricious mother, a drunken father, and a 'yellow' brother – his school days, and his first love affair, which ends in heartbreak. All through the book there is a hungry appreciation of the beauty of the world and fierce detestation of its injustice, misery and squalor. Here is a passionately earnest view of the universe. The writer seems to have flung it casually into the form of a novel.

A NOTE IN MUSIC
by Rosamund Lehmann, 1930

The author's first novel, *Dusty Answer*, was one of the most distinguished books of its season. If the present work seems to have missed distinction, it may be because the writer seems to have had a fatally good idea and invented characters to fit it, for the characters persistently behave as if they had just been invented.

THE GLASS KEY
by Dashiel Hammett, 1931

A man killed in a dark street provides the necessary corpse for this detective story which is concerned with the corruption and complications of an election in an American city. Its writing is as laconic and convincing as in that previous, much-read book, *The Maltese Falcon*, by the same author. The incidental pleasures of life described in this work are so apparently devoid of pleasure that one is compelled to the conclusion that an entirely new type of humanity is being developed in America.

SANCTUARY
by William Faulkner, 1931

This man is far and away the most important of American novelists. At the same time, I find it impossible to recommend his book indiscriminately to this genteel circulation. Faulkner is out after the biggest game, the most amorphous significances, the underlying and continuing inexpressibles. Hence, his selection of data operates in such a way as to give him the most 'significant' types of people: abnormal and deformed, half-wits, criminals, cripples; and

Top row, left, the 25-year-old Terence Rattigan, author of *French Without Tears*, 1937. Centre, poet W.H. Auden, 1935. Right, J.B. Priestley, author of *The Good Companions* and *Angel Pavement*, 1933

Bottom row, left, septuagenarian novelist H.G. Wells, 1936. Right, Dorothy Sayers, playwright and creator of Lord Peter Wimsey, 1939

Opposite, Edith Sitwell, poet and biographer of Pope, at breakfast. Cecil Beaton's portrait shows 'an interesting resemblance to certain pictures of Cowper', 1930

the most 'significant' events: crime, horror, perversion, death, and decay. This does not make for light reading. It does give those who can stand it the most intense and the noblest excitements to be found in contemporary literature.

CHRISTMAS PUDDING
by Nancy Mitford, 1932

Not for aged aunts, but certainly a gift for your sophisticated friends, is this lively account of a Christmas houseparty at Compton Bobbin, the ancestral home of the fox-hunting Lady Bobbin. The guests include all kinds of people, from the modern Glittering Young to bearded feudal cousins from Scotland. Miss Mitford keeps the whole thing going merrily with an admirable careless ease that is echoed in Mark Ogilvie Grant's amusing illustrations.

STAMBOUL TRAIN
by Graham Greene, 1932

The technique of the cinema is very adroitly adapted to the uses of the novel in this thriller, the action of which takes place on the Orient Express during its long journey between Ostend and Constantinople. Certain people scattered through the train – a chorus girl, a murderer, a political agitator, a rich Jew merchant, a woman reporter and a novelist – are the chief characters in an exciting and closely knit story.

BRAVE NEW WORLD
by Aldous Huxley, 1932

Transported to Mr. Huxley's new world one becomes very homesick for our present miseries and inconveniences. The thing is worked out with so much logic that the crowded, stan-

Top row, left to right: Laurence Housman, author of the successful play *Victoria Regina*, 1937; Clare Boothe Brokaw, playwright, 1936; Lord David Cecil, 1937; Lillian Hellman, author of *The Little Foxes*, 1937

Centre row, left, the authors Harold Nicolson and Vita Sackville-West in 1933. STEICHEN. Right, Katharine Anne Porter, writer of *Pale Horse, Pale Rider*, 1939. 'She has a style that is delicate, strong as molybdenum wire'

Bottom row, left to right: Christina Foyle, founder of book clubs and Foyle's literary luncheons, 1938; Archibald MacLeish, 'the hope of American poetry', 1934; Raymond Mortimer, essayist and critic, 1937; Sacheverell Sitwell, art critic and biographer, 1937

Right, Thomas Mann with his wife in their new house in Princeton, New Jersey, 1939. Mann was on a lecture tour of America in 1938 when Germany entered Austria. He decided not to return to his homeland. KARGER

dardised happiness of this Utopia, its clean, sterilised, calculated libertine felicity appears as the veritable approaching doom of the human race. And the scientific detail in which this world state of the future is described masks at first the book's satiric purpose as a commentary on present-day existence.

HAVE HIS CARCASE
by Dorothy Sayers, 1932
This is much more than an ordinary well-worked-out murder story – it is a witty and very entertaining novel and the novelist-detective-heroine is a pleasantly sophisticated young woman with no lugubrious nonsense about her – though a little cold-blooded at times.

TESTAMENT OF YOUTH
by Vera Brittain, 1933
Proving once again what supreme advantage truth can have over fiction, the author's straightforward story of her own life from 1900 to 1925 makes one of the season's most arresting and moving stories. This lucid and unaffected narrative, the description of the writer's own actions, endurances and emotions, and the way she makes the discoveries of youth that all human beings must make for themselves, is told with feeling but without pity. The story of the war years, the death of the man she loved, and her life as a V.A.D., is the most intensely interesting part of a book that is never dull.

A HANDFUL OF DUST
by Evelyn Waugh, 1934
One of the happy homes of England, a masterpiece of Victorian Gothic, inhabited by the country-loving Tony and his wife Brenda, is here shown in process of being devastated by the young wife's strange passion for a dismal young-man-about-town. Tragedy falls on Hetton Hall with the death of the only child of the house, and the wifeless and childless Tony removes himself to one of the outposts of Empire, where he meets with a grotesque fate. This story Mr. Waugh works out with less exuberance than in his earlier works but with a maturer irony and all that sureness of touch and caustic neatness of dialogue which place his books among the purest joys of contemporary novel-reading.

NATIONAL VELVET
by Enid Bagnold, 1935

The attraction of this book is not so much its theme of the Grand National won by a girl of fourteen on a piebald horse acquired in a shilling raffle, for this is the stuff of a schoolgirl story, but the pleasure it affords the reader of making acquaintance with the enchanting family of the Browns. Mr. Brown was the village butcher; Mrs. Brown had once swum the Channel and had since become mountainously fat. They had three beautiful daughters ranging in age from 17 to 15, a plain and bilious girl with projecting teeth, aged 14, and a little boy of four, beautiful as an angel and an engagingly accomplished liar. We really regret every minute not spent at home with the Browns.

THE CITADEL
by A. J. Cronin, 1937

At last Dr. Cronin writes a story about doctors. As usual his novel runs to a great length but there is nothing rambling about this tale of a newly fledged doctor coming to a Welsh mining village. What he found, did, and saw there is told with an unflinching regard for reality.

THE LATE GEORGE APLEY
by John P. Marquand, 1937

The gently satirical method of this 'life' of an eminent Bostonian makes a quiet but effective impression and the book is especially interesting to English people for its evocation of a genuine Boston citizen and the light it sheds on the type of fiction that is now liable to become an American best-seller.

THE YEARS
by Virginia Woolf, 1937

Subtle and unconcessive is the quality of Mrs. Woolf's mind. *The Years* presents a half-century in the undercurrent life of an English family — one of those upper-middle-class English families that spawn with the reckless immodesty popularly supposed to be the mark of the proletarian. Mrs. Woolf's book is literature, and at the same time gives the impression of music. It has nothing in common with the overstuffed family novel of Galsworthy.

AT THE MOVIES

In the Thirties, Hollywood epitomised glamour. While intellectuals and critics earnestly discussed whether films were or were not 'pure cinema', the crowds who packed the picture palaces every week – twenty million in Britain, eighty-five million in the U.S. – willingly abandoned themselves to visions of their idols, swathed in satin, chiffon, and lamé, reclining languidly on sofas, or floating in a dreamland of wide sweeping staircases, marble floors, and magnificent drawing rooms. Screen goddesses were no longer the pert little jazz babies of the Twenties, they were cool, seductive sirens with 'sex appeal'. Greta Garbo, Marlene Dietrich, Jean Harlow, and Joan Crawford headed a list of stars whose makeup, clothes, catchphrases, and every mannerism were slavishly copied by girls everywhere. 'Film is the most perfect visual medium for the exploitation of fashion and beauty that ever existed,' noted James Laver in *Vogue*. Garbo's bob, topped, after *Grand Hotel*, with a pillbox, Crawford's wide, sultry red mouth, Harlow's platinum blonde hair, Vivien Leigh's green-eyed Mediterranean colouring, Mae West's hour-glass figure, Dietrich's hollowed eyesockets and feather boas, were the trademarks of beauty. After *Morocco*, in which Dietrich played a fourth-rate music-hall singer wearing a tuxedo, girls bewailed the law that forbade women to dress as men in public.

There was plenty of adulation left over for male stars. According to *Vogue*, Robert Taylor, Clark Gable, and Tyrone Power were the top heartbreakers of the screen, with Leslie Howard, Spencer Tracy, and Robert Montgomery not far behind. 'Massed phalanxes of hysterical women' stormed the police guards at the Waldorf Astoria to get at Robert Taylor, hiding under his bed, trying to snip his hair, and hanging on to his legs when he tried to escape. Clark Gable wreaked irreparable damage to one section of the garment industry when he undressed in front of Claudette Colbert in *It Happened One Night* (1934), and revealed to shocked audiences that he didn't wear an undershirt. Sales plummeted thereafter.

The movies offered rousing entertainment. The choice was wide: historical movies, monster movies like *Dracula*, *Frankenstein*, or *King Kong*, films starring children – Shirley Temple

Right, the legendary Greta Garbo, 1932. She was M.G.M.'s trump card; she made three films a year, each one a sensation. Other actresses and audiences alike sought to emulate her fragile, fatal mystery, her melancholic gaze that said all or nothing, depending on your point of view. Under her influence hair was bobbed and voices went bass. Desperately shy, she shunned publicity. 'She has no friends, but a million fans are ready to die for her,' wrote Cecil Beaton in 1930

or Deanna Durbin – the screwball comedies of the Marx Brothers, musical spectaculars with Fred Astaire and Ginger Rogers or Jeanette Macdonald and Nelson Eddy, the films of Chaplin and Disney, family films. Realistic gangster films, like Edward G. Robinson's *Little Caesar*, *Public Enemy* with Jimmy Cagney, and *Quick Millions* with Spencer Tracy had a short heyday until suppressed by the censor as dangerous to public morals. In 1934 the Legion of Decency, horrified by the scandalous lives of some of Hollywood stars, succeeded in installing the former Postmaster General of the United States, Will Hays, as censor. Thereafter it was forbidden to show prolonged kisses, or small boys bathing naked, or characters uttering the words 'damn' or 'hell'. In bedroom scenes, the gentleman was required to keep one foot on the floor. Jean Harlow's movie *Born to be Kissed* was hastily retitled *100% Pure*, and finally released as *The Girl from Missouri*. Mae West's *It ain't*

no Sin became *I'm No Angel*.

There were a few films to make you think, like *I am a Fugitive from a Chain Gang* and *They Won't Forget*, but mostly the movies transportd you to a land of adventure and romance where there was no Recession and no threat of war, where valiant young men rose to the top and glamorous young women married the millionaire's son. Capital invested in the movies steered clear of awkward issues. The anti-war comedy *Idiot's Delight* by Robert Sherwood, in its adaptation from stage to screen, changed its location from Italy to an anonymous country where the inhabitants spoke Esperanto. In the remake of *Beau Geste* (1939), the villains were given Russian names, rather than Italian or Belgian, because film trade with Russia was very small.

In some respects Hollywood was becoming more sophisticated. Cecil Beaton spent a couple of seasons there and sent back bulletins for *Vogue*. 'Can it be that good taste is coming

Right, another European import, Marlene Dietrich, seductive in Schiaparelli's Russian furs, 1936. 'Dietrich is Paramount's Garbo, and has Garbo's eyes, a husky voice, and a long contract,' wrote *Vogue* in 1933. The daughter of a Prussian policeman, she became famous for her part as Lola in Von Sternberg's *The Blue Angel*, 1932. She brought a glamour to the suspenders, feather boas, and men's evening dress of her wicked-romantic underworld roles. She made slacks fashionable. CECIL BEATON

Left, Merle Oberon dressed as Messalina for her part in Korda's film of Robert Graves's *I, Claudius* with Charles Laughton, 1937

Right, Claudette Colbert photographed on the set of *Cleopatra* by Hoyningen-Huené, 1934

Below left, Norma Shearer, star of *Strange Interlude* and wife of producer Irving Thalberg, 1932.
STEICHEN

Below, Carole Lombard, in a gown of Bianchini's rose and silver lamé, 1934. She was married to Clark Gable and was killed in a plane crash on her way to meet him.
HOYNINGEN-HUENE

Facing page, Katharine Hepburn as the eponymous heroine in *Mary of Scotland*, 1936.
BRUEHL-BOURGES

into the movies?' he asked in 1931, noting that in movies of baronial halls, ladies did not wear the lowest of tulle evening gowns for breakfast any more, and that Lady Maureen Stanley had been hired to advise on matters of taste and etiquette for a social comedy.

The big breakthrough in the Thirties was colour – 'as bilious and crude as the coloured photographs in ancient railway carriages,' wrote *Vogue*. However it could make a triumph of even second-rate films. The colour photography of animated cartoons was technically simpler than that of natural scenery, and Walt Disney used it particularly successfully in his *Silly Symphonies*, in which flowers burst open, frogs hopped, and insects swirled to the music of Mendelssohn's *Spring Song*. *Snow White* came out in January 1938 and *Vogue* choked over its 'saccharine pixiedom', but the tough columnist Westbrook Pegler dubbed it 'the happiest thing that has happened in this world since the Armistice.' It set the U.S. humming 'Heigh Ho' and kept a toy factory working 24 hours a day for months trying to keep up with the demand for rubber models of Dopey and the other dwarfs.

Hollywood with its vast resources and salaries lured talented actors and screenwriters from the stage, and from Europe. Edna Best, Leslie Howard, Vivien Leigh, Diana Wynyard, and many others all crossed the Atlantic. The British studios at Elstree, Denham, Teddington, and Ealing could not really compete, in spite of the skill of directors like Alfred Hitchcock and Carol Reed. 'Hitch' himself, maker of electric thrillers like *The 39 Steps*, *The Man who knew Too Much*, and *The Lady Vanishes*, was also lured to Hollywood, to make *Rebecca*. The Hungarian Alexander Korda's company London Films did produce several successful movies, particularly *The Private Life of Henry VIII*, *Rembrandt* (which made stars of Charles Laughton and Korda's wife Merle Oberon) and *Catherine the Great* with Flora Robson. George Bernard Shaw made his debut in the movies: he adapted his play *Pygmalion*, and won the American Academy of Motion Pictures Award for best scenario. Leslie Howard and Wendy Hiller took the leads.

Intellectual Russian and German films were no longer fashionable, although people enjoyed Fritz Lang's *M* and fearfully watched Leni

Left, Joan Crawford, 1938. Women everywhere copied her bow-tie mouth and padded shoulders. HORST

Below right, Mae West in *She Done Him Wrong*, 1933. 'This amply cushioned lady of the yellow hair and the leering lip has *It* to an overpowering extent,' wrote *Vogue*. The first actress to make fun of sex, she said, 'I didn't discover curves, I only uncovered them,' and claimed that as a child she spread coconut oil on those areas of her body that she wished to 'attain prominence'

Far right, Paulette Goddard, the gamine of *Modern Times*, in Jaeckel's dazzling white fox coat, 1936. This was the last film in which Chaplin played the little tramp; already he was being accused of moral turpitude and Communist sympathies. HURRELL

Riefenstahl's portrayal of the new Germany in *The Triumph of the Will*, and her record of the 1936 Olympic games. French films by directors like René Clair, Sacha Guitry, and Jacques Feyder were admired for their intelligence, wit, and subtlety. Julien Duvivier's *Un Carnet de Bal* tells the touching story of what happened to the young men who signed a girl's dance card, while Jean Renoir's *La Grande Illusion*, starring Erich von Stroheim, and made in 1937, remains one of the most compassionate studies ever made of people in time of war.

The decade opened with Garbo's first talkie *Anna Christie* in 1930 (GARBO TALKS ran the billboards), and ended with her only comedy *Ninotchka*, in which she played a Russian spy (GARBO LAUGHS). Two years later she retired for good. In between, Hollywood's Golden Age produced a list of classic films that still draw audiences today: *The Wizard of Oz, City Lights, The Blue Angel, The Invisible Man, The Prisoner of Zenda, Wuthering Heights, Hellzapoppin', A Night at the Opera* . . . and especially *Gone With the Wind*.

99

CONSTANCE BENNETT

KATHARINE HEPBURN

MIRIAM HOPKINS

RONALD COLMAN

GARY COOPER

CLARK GABLE

JOAN CRAWFORD

JEAN HARLOW

WILLIAM POWELL

FREDRIC MARCH

WARNER BAXTER

TALLULAH BANKHEAD

CLAUDETTE COLBERT

BETTE DAVIS

MARGARET SULLAVAN

WHO'LL PLAY RHETT AND SCARLETT?

The casting of the film version of Margaret Mitchell's bestseller *Gone with the Wind* created breathless speculation. Two hundred thousand people wrote to MGM giving their suggestions. Every actress except Garbo was reputed to be angling for the part of Scarlett O'Hara. Fourteen hundred girls were interviewed and ninety screen-tested but the producers seemed unable to find anyone suitable. 'Because Scarlett O'Hara is what some call a bitch, it appears almost impossible to cast the role satisfactorily, though I would have thought it would be quite a simple matter in Hollywood or elsewhere,' wrote *Vogue*'s acerbic Lesley Blanch. The magazine fanned the flames with an article and innovative identikit pictures of Rhett and Scarlett made by superimposing the photos of many of the hopefuls.

The film took three years and $4,250,000 to make and passed through the hands of 13 scenario writers and three directors. It brought the Golden Age of Hollywood to a sweeping climax when it opened in Atlanta in December 1939.

Right, Vivien Leigh. 'It is time the "fame-in-a-night" girl gave us something more than dazzling beauty and a photogenique home life,' wrote *Vogue* in 1937. By 1939, she had. A minor English actress, she was offered a screen test for the part of Scarlett in *Gone with the Wind* while on a visit to Hollywood, and was signed up immediately. She got down a Southern drawl in three days

Left, *Vogue*'s composite pictures of how Rhett and Scarlett might look, made up of photos of the actors and actresses aspiring to the parts. Many unknown Southern belles also begged for the chance to play Scarlett

Right, Robert Taylor, 'this year's public heart-throb No. 1', 1937

Far right, 'Hollywood's darling', Henry Fonda, star of *The Moon's our Home* and *Jesse James*, 1938

Below, Gary Cooper, star of *Mr Deeds Goes to Town*, in which he played a small-town man who inherits 20 million dollars. He gives it away, and is therefore charged with lunacy, 1938.
HORST

Above right, Douglas Fairbanks Jr., 1934

Below right, swashbuckler Errol Flynn, 1936

Far right, British-born cinema star Madeleine Carroll, modelling a Chanel dress, 1937. Her publicity made much of the fact that she was a graduate of Birmingham University and was married to Guardsman Philip Astley – although it did not mention that her husband had to resign his commission for marrying an actress. She starred in *The General Died at Dawn* with Gary Cooper and *The Prisoner of Zenda* with Douglas Fairbanks Jr. HORST

Left, a scene from Walter Wanger's film *Vogues of 1938*, showing actresses waiting for their cues in arm-stalls, 'necessary precaution against the least wrinkle, the slightest crease'

Right, 'We love Benny Goodman (far left), who put swing in Carnegie Hall with 'Yellow Dog Blues'. Ginger Rogers and Fred Astaire, dancing frenetically. Orson Welles, who produced the sceneryless *Julius Caesar*. Robert Taylor's profile. Lily Pons, the Metropolitan's streamlined soprano. Salvador Dali, chic Spanish painter of melted gold watches and dead fish. Alfred Lunt and Lynn Fontanne. Walt Disney, king of beasts. Dorothy Thompson (prone), militant oracle of the syndicated column. And aloft, America's sweetheart, Shirley Temple. Drawing by Covarrubias, 1938

A PRIMER OF ART

'A lady of quality,' wrote *Vogue* in 1936, 'should be able to walk into any drawing room, to look at the picture over the mantelpiece and to exclaim: 'Oh, what a charming Picasso of the early Blue Period', or 'I like your new Follower of Massaccio (circa 1420) immensely'.

'If she guesses right, she is a gentleman and a scholar. If she is wrong, her cultural standing is usually sadly impaired. It is more dangerous to be wrong about the author of a modern painting than of an old one. If you mistake Quentin Latour for Fantin Latour, you can laugh it off; but God help you, if you cannot tell Braque from Brook.

'*Vogue* offers you, through these paintings by Miguel Covarrubias, an infallible means of recognizing at sight the works of six important modern painters. Our system is easy, making you remember the unfamiliar by comparing it with the familiar. The technicalities of painting do not enter into it. You have only to distinguish between a delicatessen and an ironmonger's shop. This is not too much to ask, is it?'

1. PICASSO usually looks like a display room in a RUG AND QUILT department. Of course Picasso has many periods – but so have the quilts and rugs. Some periods look like crazy quilts; the others like afghans or hooked rugs, or even modernistic rugs. The rug illustrated here can be turned upside down – and this only improves the design (try it if you don't believe us). A real connoisseur of course should be able to recognize a Picasso even right side up

2. BRAQUE is best described as a window in a DELICATESSEN STORE. There is always food in his paintings (not always appetizing, though). Some of his paintings look strangely Picasso-ish – rugs with lots of food in them, as it were. There is a legend, fairly current, that Braque once asked Picasso, pointing at a picture in an exhibition: 'I do not remember whether this is your painting or mine. Do you?' To which Picasso wittily replied, 'No!'

3. LEGER can be remembered easily if you keep in mind IRONMONGERS' SHOPS. Some of his compositions are also reminiscent of locksmiths' supplies. He has kitchenware in his paintings, and ladies surrounded by ironmongery, but the ladies in this case are made out of stovepipes

4. DALI prefers for his pictures the atmosphere of an ORTHOPAEDIC SHOP. He paints with the precision of a catalogue: general hospital supplies, trusses, crutches, arch-supporters, and bandages, with an occasional tibia bone or bunion-remover set thrown in. When in cheerful mood – he wasn't here – he might decorate a tumour with roses. People in his paintings are sometimes so ruptured and crippled that they are reduced to a mere rib chop

5. DE CHIRICO groups together objects that can usually be found in an ANTIQUE SHOP or even a junk shop. Whenever you see a picture with a Greek plaster statue, a football, and a paperweight horse in it, you can safely call it 'an early Chirico'. The horse may become a zebra, but do not let this deter you

6. MATISSE is easy to recognize because his paintings always look like a REMNANT COUNTER, full of bargains in chintz, prints, and Paisley – bright, cheerful, and inexpensive. His models (regardless of dress) have the peculiarly disinterested look of shop assistants at remnant counters during sale time

1

2

3

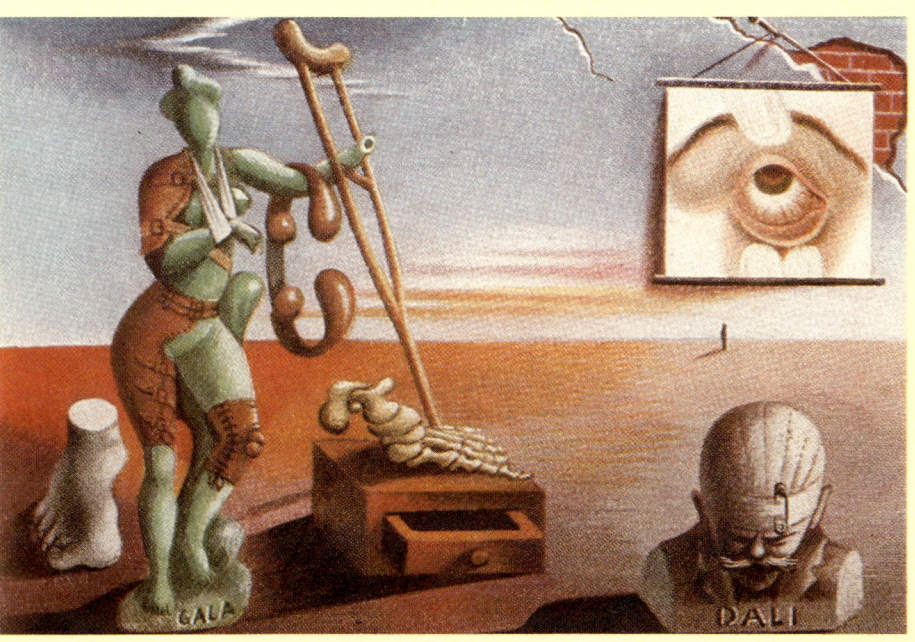

4

5

6

SURREALISM

Left, *Vogue* cover by Salvador Dali, June 1939

Below right, Dali, posing with the diving mask he wore at the opening of the Surrealist Exhibition in Burlington House in 1936. It was supposed to symbolize plumbing the depths of the subconscious, but he almost asphyxiated in it.
CECIL BEATON

Far right, 'I dream about an evening dress'; painting by Dali for *Vogue*, 1937

In 1936, 10 years after the Surrealist manifesto, the first Surrealism Exhibition was held in England at Burlington House. It attracted 20,000 people and was followed by an even larger one in New York. Salvador Dali, the movement's most outrageous exponent, delivered the opening speech of the Exhibition dressed in a diving suit, and nearly smothered to death because someone forgot to open the air valve. The suit, *Vogue* explained in an article in defence of Surrealism, was supposed to symbolise the descent to the lower depths of the subconscious. Surrealism was 'Dada with a dash of Freud ... You know the old formula: 'Man Bites Dog'? — only in this case the Dog has Paranoia, and the Man is really a couple of other guys.' Dali received reporters sitting on his desk on top of a bed with all the lampshades turned upside down, or on less formal occasions wearing a loaf of bread on his head.

The work of the Surrealists — among them de Chirico, Dali, and Pierre Roy — with its meticulously realistic portrayal of the mysterious disorder of the unconscious mind, still sent dinner parties into whoops, but its influence was felt everywhere. There were Surrealist ballets, Surrealist fashions, including suits by Schiaparelli with bureau drawers for pockets, and fashion pictures in *Vogue* of ladies in

Left, the surrealist painter Pavel Tchelichev at work, 1938

Top right, a Bergdorf Goodman window showing a Surrealist influence, 1938

Centre right, bottom left and below, exhibits at the Paris Surrealist Exhibition, 1938: André Masson's birdcage muzzle, a plaster phonograph with assorted extremities, and Dali's famous red-lips sofa

Facing page, not exactly Surreal, but other-worldly; Henri Matisse tending his collection of rare birds, 1938

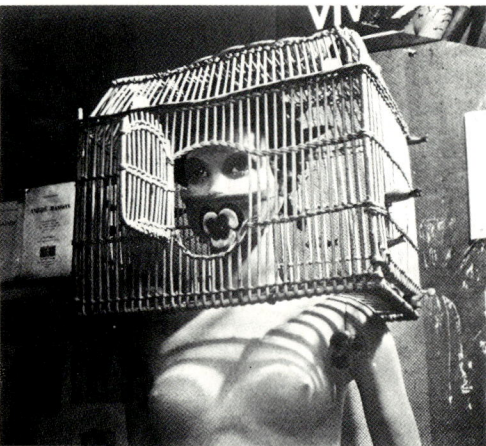

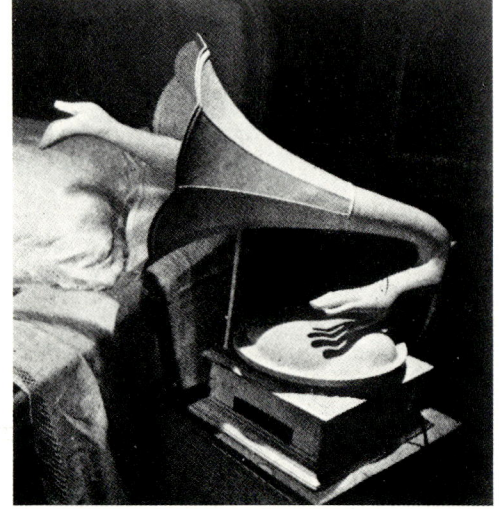

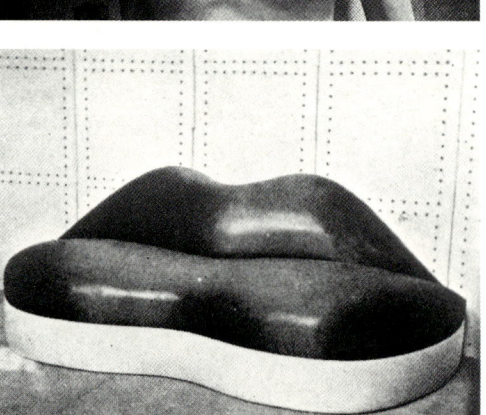

evening dresses holding their own cut-off heads or sitting on garbage heaps. There were Surrealist movies, in which you could see, among other things, a cow, sleeping luxuriously in a Louis XVI bed; an ox-cart driving through a Louis XIV salon; a man kicking a blind beggar; a priest dragging a baby grand piano with two dead mules attached to it; and a burning tree, a giraffe, and a plough being thrown out of a window.

There was even a Surrealist ball. The programme was illustrated by a Dali drawing of a lady with snails instead of feet and a pram instead of a head. Mme Dali wore a skull cap with enormous black wings, a baby's head covered in blood and flies, and a lobster with gloves. She was said to represent Necrophilia.

STYLE AT HOME

'Where are the snow-white rooms of yesteryear' asked *Vogue* in 1938. Syrie Maugham's famous white drawing room had become a red and white room – although lilies were still everywhere. Her new country house, a turreted Victorian fantasy at Ethrope Park, was decorated with flowered wallpapers, chintzes, and the new American Venetian blinds. 'Gaiety is the new note in decoration.' She also introduced the corner sofa, which split into two separate pieces of furniture if necessary – 'a wise precaution in these days when people move on'.

For the lifestyle of the Thirties was changing: the Depression forced people to move into flats or close up part of their houses, and to do without servants. In 1931 Mies van der Rohe, Director of the Bauhaus at Dessau, organised an exhibition in Berlin entitled 'The Dwelling House of Today', which reflected the new move to simplicity. It showed life-sized houses by such architects and designers as Walter Gropius, Marcel Breuer, and Jan Ruhtenberg. In actuality, Mies claimed, the modern house did not yet exist – that is, one built in accordance with contemporary tastes and habits, that had rid itself of traditional outmoded forms and irrelevant decoration. His own inexpensively built, one-storey example had an 'immaculate simplicity'; indoors and outdoors connected by means of great windows and unbroken walls to give ample sun, air, and space. He used only the essentials of furniture: beds, chairs, and tables, in the most elegant materials possible, with sculpture, books, flowers, and *objects d'art* achieving colour, individuality, and intimacy, and proving that simplicity need not entail drab standardisation. 'The immediate reaction is to want one like it,' wrote *Vogue*.

'Stream-line' became a buzz word of Thirties' design. It was even the title of one of C. B. Cochran's revues. Art Deco, the modern style that was crystallized in the Paris Exposition Internationale des Arts Decoratifs et Industriels Modernes in 1925, had come to mean a 'stream-lined' functionalism, incorporating such design features as plate-glass windows, strip lighting, mirror glass to make rooms seem larger, and no knick-knacks. 'The most successful feature of modern decoration,' wrote *Vogue*, was concealed lighting. Central heating was still in its troubled infancy in Britain, although they had got it right in America. Mrs. Simpson's first conversation with the Prince of Wales is said to have been about central heating. He introduced the subject, to which she replied, 'I had hoped for more from the Prince of Wales.'

The Prince himself turned to Lady Mendl to decorate his beloved Fort Belvedere and the royal yachts. The famous American-born hostess was said to have invented the profession of interior decoration in her young days – 'a new and necessary profession for women of taste'. She did two of the rooms at the Fort in plaster relief, which was 'all the rage'.

Vogue itself advised eclecticism rather than correctness and adherence to one particular style. Certainly the celebrities' homes that appeared in its pages were varied. Lord and Lady Mountbatten's penthouse duplex at the top of the new Brook House on Park Lane had a cinema – 'a cinema installation is now one of those things that no properly equipped modern house lacks' – and Edwina's bedroom was decorated by Rex Whistler. (Lord Louis's was designed as a ship's cabin with portholes giving on to Monte Carlo harbour.) Norma Shearer's house in California also had projection panels in the living room. Cole Porter's silver lacquer and zebra-skin-rugged music room was the essence of Art Deco, Gary Cooper's house showed a Japanese influence, while Jascha Heifetz indulged himself with a brightly coloured bemuralled bar.

Facing page, above, the living room of the 'modernist' house belonging to the headmaster of Dartington Hall School, designed by Howe and Lescaze, 1934

Below, the New York apartment of architect Philip Johnson, designed by Mies van der Rohe, 1931

Above, a golden spiral staircase in the Paris apartment of Charles de Beistegui, designed by Le Corbusier, 1932. Its clean lines contrast oddly with the period furniture

Left, the roof terrace of M de Beistegui's apartment; when required, the hedges were rolled back and folded up electrically, to give magnificent views of Paris

Top, the entrance hall of the Mountbattens' new penthouse, 1937

Above, Lady Beatty's tentlike dining room, by Sibyl Colefax and John Fowler, 1939

Top right, Syrie Maugham's bird's-egg blue dining room with palm tree motifs at her new country house, 1936

Right, Mrs Maugham in her London house, 1934.
CECIL BEATON

Above left, Cecil Beaton's bathroom became a witty guestbook: he outlined his guests' hands with a brush and had them sign their palms, 1932

Left, Jascha Heifetz' bar, decorated with yellow, white, brown, and red murals caricaturing amusing episodes in his life, 1936

Above, zebra skins, white leather sofas, and silver lacquer decorate Cole Porter's music room in his Paris home, 1933

Right, Mrs Dudley Ward – former friend of the Prince of Wales – had her new house in Avenue Road remodelled after her own ideas, and executed by Marion Dorn and Doris Robertson: lots of white, herring-bone tweed upholstery, vermilion velvet curtains, and 'a new type of carpet, white and curly like lamb's wool', 1934

MADAM TRIES HER HAND

Informality and simplicity were becoming the keynotes of entertaining. 'Nobody has 'grand food' any more. Lunching at Lady Colefax's house, we had a huge dish of macaroni done with cream and cheese, lamb with mint sauce, potato croquettes and spinach, and an apple charlotte with cream. I believe it is the only kind of food one really likes now.' Liveried footmen were *démodé*, except in great houses, and rustic tableware – wood, pottery and baskets – were suddenly smart. Cocktail parties, by contrast, had become very substantial, with trays of enticing food, so that you could fortify yourself before the theatre and have a good supper afterwards. 'I wonder if dinner is disappearing from our social scheme of life,' asked *Vogue*. 'And what if it does – for is not dinner a very pompous meal, and have we not passed the pompous period?'

Mrs. Simpson's cocktails made news: 'Listen to this – peeled grapes filled with cheese, with toothpicks stuck through them; hot American soda biscuits filled with cod's roe or crisp bacon and hot chutney; cornucopias of Prague ham filled with a creamy mixture of cheese; hot fish cakes and what appear to be little welsh rarebits on toast; these are some of the excellent things that Mrs. Ernest Simpson serves with cocktails. And she makes her own cocktails on a tray in front of her on a low table with the same ease as if she were pouring tea. I find it a very graceful gesture.'

The idea of doing things yourself – especially when it wasn't absolutely necessary – was one of the best entertainment turns. After-theatre 'nightcaps' – servantless, buffet-style suppers – or frying eggs and bacon in the small hours were delightfully novel. In Paris, ladies went a step further. It was no longer enough to have morning discussions with your cook: you actually took a hand in the kitchen. 'Maybe Colette started it,' suggested *Vogue*, 'apron tied round her waist and contentment on her face, as she prepares the *galettes* and *vin chaud* for her tea-parties. At any rate, cooking has become the new social accomplishment of Paris. The great national talent is replacing politics, the ballet, and even the *'vie intérieur'* as a dinner-table subject.' Enthusiasts trekked to the Sorbonne for lessons. Mrs. Reginald Fellowes had a little kitchen built in next to her sitting room, while André Dubonnet's new 'super-

Above, my Lady in the kitchen, 1934

Above right, Comtesse Alexandre de Casteja handles a crisis. Centre, Colette watches the pot. Below, 'Comtesse Charles de Polignac stirs them up', 1935

Facing page, the new informality in dining: Parisian 'picnic' dinners. Dresses by Mainbocher and Molyneux, 1932. HOYNINGEN-HUENE

kitchen' was invaded nightly by guests begging to be allowed to help. Many celebrities published their specialities in *Vogue*.

Colette's Truffles au Champagne
Use a little over a pound of truffles to half a bottle of champagne.

Clean the truffles well and peel them. Season with pepper and salt and cook for 20 minutes in the champagne in a covered saucepan, together with a *mirepoix* sauce. (This is composed of one carrot, one onion, one stem of parsley, a pinch of thyme, and a bay leaf, cooked together with a very small amount of water). Remove truffles, keeping them covered and hot, and cook the sauce and champagne mixture again to reduce it to a quarter of its original quantity. Drain the juice and pour over the truffles before serving.

Lewis Mumford's Devilled Crabs
Soak medium-sized hard crabs in salt water for half an hour, then plunge into hot water and boil for 12 to 15 minutes. When cold, remove lungs, legs, and claws, and collect all the edible meat. Clean and dry the shells.

Finely chop two small white oinons, and sauté for a few minutes with half a green pepper, chopped. Do not brown. Add half a pound of chopped mushrooms, and continue to sauté for ten minutes.

Make a roux with two ounces butter and sufficient flour to make a creamy consistency. Add milk to thin a little, then the onion mixture, salt, cayenne pepper, a little nutmeg, and some finely chopped parsley. Add two raw egg yolks and mix in the crab meat. Place the mixture in the dry crab shells. Cover with breadcrumbs, paprika, and knobs of butter. Bake for 15 minutes.

Devilled crabs are better if prepared six to 12 hours before serving.

Alfred Lunt's Corned Beef Hash
Chop together corned beef and hot, freshly boiled potatoes very finely, using twice as much meat as potatoes. Season with salt and pepper. Add grated onion and fry in hot butter in a frying pan. Turn down the heat and cook slowly, adding cream now and then to keep the hash moist. Serve with poached eggs and a sauce made of thin mayonnaise and grated fresh horseradish. Serve the sauce separately.

Mrs. Reed Vreeland's Fish Soufflé
Make a roux with two ounces of butter and a tablespoonful of flour. Add half a cup of milk to make a stiff sauce, and then the finely broken flesh of two whitings. Flavour with salt, pepper, and a teaspoon of anchovy essence. Beat the whites of two eggs stiffly, and mix well into the mixture. Steam for 20 minutes. Serve with mushroom sauce in a sauceboat.

Syrie Maugham's Haddock Pancakes
Remove the skin and bones from a finely cured finnan haddock, chop finely, and cook in cream

and butter. Make pancakes with four ounces flour, half a pint of milk, two eggs, and a pinch of salt. Immediately they are cooked, stuff with haddock mixture, and serve piping hot.

Lady Colefax's Iced Summer Pudding
Line a mould with thin pieces of bread so they overlap each other, and place a thin slice at the bottom of the dish. Boil any soft fruit with sugar until very soft, and fill the dish, layering the fruit with bread until the dish is full. Press the dish with a weight, and place on ice to chill. To serve, unmould and pour over raspberry or blackcurrant fool. Serve with cream.

FAR AND WIDE

'The flight from England is at its height,' wrote *Vogue* in 1938. 'By pullman, plane and 'cruiser', all who can are leaving us, and departures from town have all the finality of the end of a Victorian July. Mayfair and Manhattan meet by the blue seas of Florida, Jamaica and Ceylon, enjoy Mexican baroque, the joys of Copacabana, the terrace at Shepheard's and the garden at the Mount Nelson. The Riviera seems next-door these days and Switzerland is most people's tonic – but this is hardly travel. No longer do we get letters from Cannes (remember the gay villa life in the Twenties?) which always commenced, even if there were a snowstorm, by the classic 'as I write, the smell of orange blossom . . .' Nothing less than a cactus landscape or an adobe village excites us now.

'As to once mythical Bali, where the Duchess of Sutherland, Sir Anthony Weldon and others are about to arrive, they say to you, 'Of course you've been to Bali, but which year?' (Covarrubias' book on Bali is the year's loveliest travel book.) But whatever point our friends reach on the social globe, nothing will prevent them from sending home shoals of postcards by expensive air-mail, hoping that these will reach us in a fog. But our revenge comes later when the travellers return. Shall we listen to their eager tales? We shall not . . .'

Above, Mrs Harrison Williams, Countess Edith di Zoppola, Mrs Robert McAdoo and **friends scale a temple in Mexico, 1936. CECIL BEATON**

Left, hunting giraffe in Kenya with a 'boy', 1936

Above left, cocktail hour in Fez: a sherif entertains his European guests on cushions around a low table to eat Moroccan delicacies out of a big bowl. Sketch by Carl Erickson, 1931

Above, a circle of hunters closing in after a successful tiger hunt, 1935

Far left, Mr and Mrs Vanderbilt being welcomed in Palm Island, 1932

Left, keeping cool in a Patou dress designed to be worn under African skies, 1931

Below, river travel in darkest Africa, 1935

Right, 'Mme Corniglion copes with the transport of her car across one of the tributaries of the Niger,' 1931

Up and away

'Heston aerodrome, that power-station of contemporary civilisation, is rapidly becoming the new nerve centre for English social life,' reported *Vogue* in 1934. In the Thirties, everyone was learning to fly. Lady Londonderry could often be seen lunching in the restaurant at Heston before her afternoon lesson, while plenty of ladies in America could come up with the $700 you needed to rent a plane and get your licence. Mrs. Joseph Brooks owned a Bellanca, while Mrs. Richard Du Pont had a silver glider. 'Flying belongs to the twentieth century and everyone in it.'

The passion for flying was fuelled by the glamorous exploits of women like Amy Johnson, a fish merchant's daughter from Hull, who in 1930 set off to fly solo to Australia with a packet of sandwiches and a thermos of tea. She completed the trip in 19½ days, despite many emergency landings, and at one stage having to repair wing damage with sticking plaster. In 1932 the American Amelia Earhart became the first woman to fly the Atlantic solo, in 13½ hours. 'Amelia Earhart thinks that women are on equal flying terms with men,' reported *Vogue*. Earhart disappeared over the South Pacific two years later, during a round-the-world trip. Men on occasion also grabbed the headlines. Howard Hughes flew round the world in three days 19 hours and 10 seconds (!) in 1938. Even Douglas Corrigan, who started off from Long Island for California in an antiquated plane but went in the wrong direction and ended up in Ireland, was cheered like a hero.

Of even more interest to *Vogue* readers than records was what women flyers wore. Mrs. Lindbergh favoured a white canvas helmet – 'good for the South' – and a double-breasted leather jacket from Abercrombie and Fitch.

Commercial flying was expanding rapidly. Planes were larger and more comfortable, with gangways, more headroom, buffet meals, and stewards to take care of you. Many of Europe's major cities were linked by air routes. London to Paris took a little over three hours, but longer distances were also becoming more commonplace. *Vogue* showed Katherine Hepburn alighting from a 'breathless hop' of 19½ hours from California to New York. Mrs. Henry Luce had a gold cigarette case etched with a map of the United States, with rubies marking the important airports.

The airship *Hindenburg* plied the Atlantic in 1936 but when it caught fire the following year zeppelin travel came to a tragic end. It was succeeded by the new Pan Am clippers, eighty-five feet long, with lounges decorated by Norman Bel Geddes. Mrs. Cornelius Vanderbilt Whitney, wife of Pan Am's chairman, reported in *Vogue* on the first transatlantic flight in 1939. In particular she praised the perfect beds and the five-course dinner of fruit cocktail, hot consommé, chicken, ham, mushrooms and potatoes, asparagus with hollandaise, and strawberry shortcake, and remarked that, 'It occurred to no-one to dress for dinner.'

Far left, the Air France aeroplane arrives at Le Bourget, 1938. 'Thanks to air travel, London has become a sort of suburb of Paris, and Paris a suburb of London; shopping in Bond Street alternates with the Faubourg Saint-Honoré.' SCHALL

Left, Amy Mollison, *née* Johnson, poses 'with nonchalant chic' on the B.A.Eagle she flew for the King's cup, 1936. 'She dresses for record breaking as if for a lunch date.' After her triumphant solo flight to Australia in a secondhand Gipsy Moth in 1930, she was awarded the C.B.E., and cheering crowds on the streets of London gave her a heroine's welcome. Her marriage to fellow pilot Jim Mollison was shortlived. SCHALL

Right, the perfect outfit for the traveller: a navy blue linen suit with a three-quarter cape and a white linen hat and scarf, by Aquascutum, 1934

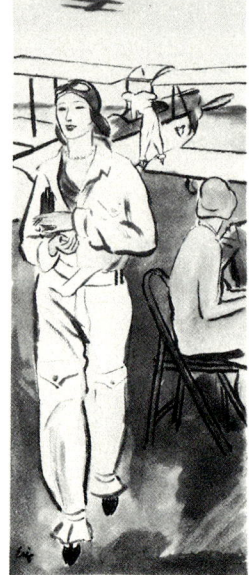

Above, Amelia Earhart, 'spanner of oceans and continents', checks a propeller, 1933. The previous year, she became the first woman to fly the Atlantic solo, making the trip from Newfoundland to Ireland in 13½ hours

Right, 'dropping down for tea on Long Island', 1930

Far left, 'Mr and Mrs Horatio S. Shonnard Jr., and the Sikorsky S38 seaplane that is their chief means of transportation on Long Island and in Florida,' 1938

Left, Jacqueline Cochran, holder of many aviation records, including the women's world speed record, 1938. A former nurse, she won her licence during a three-week holiday. Her apartment contained a floor-sized compass and the fuel-tank of her record-breaking Seversky. TONI FRISSEL

Below left, Katharine Hepburn alighting after her 'breathless' coast to coast hop of 19½ hours, 1934

Right, *Vogue* embraces the flying craze on a cover, 1937. BRUEHL

All at sea

Right, 'Marine life from A to E' Drawing by Alajálov, 1936

Far right, *Vogue*'s-eye-view of Boat Manners, 1936

NOTICE TO PASSENGERS!

REGULATIONS TO BE OBSERVED WHILE
EMBARKING AND ON BOARD SHIP
(ANY SHIP)

1. Don't let people you're very attached to hang around for hours saying good-bye

2. Don't condemn your fellow passengers because of the faces you see at the embarkation

3. Don't change into shorts, slacks, and halters the minute the boat leaves Quarantine

4. Don't speak to men in
   a. Caps   b. Plus-fours   c. Sweaters with initials

5. Don't speak to women
   a. At all

6. Don't think you have to wear your orchids to dinner every night

7. Don't cling to the outmoded custom of not dressing the first night out. If you've had time to unpack, there's no reason for not changing for dinner

8. Don't stuff yourself with crêpes Suzette, caviar, and pâté de foie gras just because they're on the bill of fare

9. Don't keep crabbing about
   a. The customs   b. The rate of exchange   c. The Awful People

10. Don't forget that the sweeping vistas of a big liner are an ideal background for
    a. Floral head-dresses (see page 44)
    b. Little fur wraps (see page 45)

11. Don't ask the Captain   b. Whether he expects fog
    a. What time the ship docks
    c. If he ever gets tired of the sea

12. Don't make cock-sure pronouncements on international affairs to reporters when all they want is your picture

MAIDEN VOYAGE

Far left, passengers at one of their favourite occupations

Left, a corner of the sports deck

Below left, passengers fight fat in the super-gymnasium

Right, Lord and Lady Milford Haven relaxing

Drawings by Cecil Beaton

by Cecil Beaton, 1936

The May trees were in blossom. All roads to Southampton were busy with a stream of cars speeding to the *Queen Mary*. On the dock, a large yellow caterpillar, the awninged gang-plank, led to the new monster ship, with its Hieronymus Bosch inferno of activity. Here, in the electric light, it could be any time of the day or night in any country, for the crowds, swarming like excited ants to inspect the vessel, were of every nationality. Along, up, down, the crowds bustled, while stewards shouted, 'keep moving, please'. To spread pandemonium among the ants, sirens went off, hooters and fog horns were blown, bells clanged, and after the hurried leave-takings the boat was launched on its historic career.

Aeroplanes roared above, the pearl-coloured funnels rent the earth with their hoots. Photographers clicked their lenses and cinema men ground the wheels of the 'eyes of the world', while the thousands on board waved to the greater thousands on land. The black-and-gold-uniformed band clashed out the anthem – 'Britannia Rules the Waves'.

Gradually the boats in the sea become distant specks and the vast crowds aboard move in droves seeing the beauties and magnificences of England's latest pride and joy. They swarm round the swimming pool, into the vast lounges, in cocktail bars, smoke rooms, children's playgrounds, dog kennels, private dining-rooms, drawing rooms, massage and writing rooms. Eventually, exhausted, they settle down to rest and while away the time as on any other Atlantic crossing. The men bring out their pipes, women their shorts and sailor trousers. Everyone eats enormously, socialises a lot, and there is leonine prowling of the decks and greed for excercise, since this is a British boat. But the zephyrs from the sea overcome all, and cause their victims to lie in crazed positions drugged by sleep, mouths open, hats knocked sideways; one man a lighted cigarette still on his sagging lower lip.

Every public room is always filled to over-flowing. The writing desks are never innocent of souvenir collectors, and after the second day the company's supply of 25,000 postcards is exhausted. The ink runs low in the wells, and stamps give out entirely. At night, the betting on the run of the ship reaches great heights; the value of the pool reaches four figures. There are hordes of autograph hunters, and Miss Frances Day, the English musical comedy blonde, in a cute tam o'shanter, sailor suit, inturned toes and moueing lips, poses on the sun deck sucking an orangeade through a straw for a dozen amateur photographers. The startlingly blonde cinema actress, Miss Anita Louise, makes a lovely entrance for dinner in 'Midsummer Night's Dream' draperies. Mr. Peter Fleming calmly writes reports to *The Times*, oblivious of the hysteria caused by the hitches in the radio rooms.

When constructing a boat, even a luxury liner, the English do not consider their women very carefully. There are hardly any large mirrors in the general room, no great flight of stairs for ladies to make an entrance. The decorations have a monotony: there is too much woodwork. The main lounge sadly misses the discarded Duncan Grant mural, and the Wadsworth surrealism does not look well in close juxtaposition with the bronze pilasters of Renaissance knights in the smoking lounge. The Verandah Grill is the prettiest room on any ship – becomingly lit, gay in colour, and so successful that it would be crowded if twice its present size. The cabins are beautifully equipped and more refreshingly decorated than on any other boat. There are fewer paper-cap galas than on a French boat, and sportsmen are taken greater care of with squash courts, pools, deck tennis and the excitement of the afternoon horse-racing.

The approach to New York was deeply moving. Aeroplanes roared past the portholes. Stewards fidgeted about the luggage. Screams of hooters, roars of engines, cheers, and the clash of bands. The aeroplanes swooped with deafening noise to drop roses. A Versailles *grands eaux* effect was produced by the fountains of fire boats. From every window kisses were blown and handkerchiefs waved, and the cheers reverberated from the skycrapers.

The air was filled with confetti. Along the Battery, the crowds had been standing since day-light, forty deep. New York, appreciative of all achievement, gave a magnificent welcome to the *Queen Mary*.

THE NEW YORK WORLD'S FAIR

In April 1939, in the teeth of an arming Europe, the New York World's Fair, dedicated to 'a happier way of American living', was declared open. *Vogue* called this colossal extravaganza of fireworks, exhibitions, and fun 'the Coney Island of the intelligentsia'. The 700-foot Trylon and vast Perisphere, dramatic symbols of the Fair, loomed over its 1200 acres of Flushing Meadow, upon which stood whole cities and civilisations of the future. No-one overlooked the irony of the grandiosely named Court of Peace lying nearly a mile from the Plaza of Foreign Pavilions, nor that of the Lagoon of Nations being fringed by weeping willows.

'Democracity', a diorama-music-voice-movie show within the Perisphere, gave you the World of Tomorrow, with conveyor belts of seats transporting you through the landscape of 1960 as seen by Norman Bel Geddes. There was a rocket airport and a 'vodor' – a vocal robot which sounded like a man with a harelip. A time capsule was buried, containing amongst its treasures a copy of *Gone With the Wind*, a picture of Jesse Owens winning the 100 metres, and the Lord's Prayer in 300 languages.

Everywhere were up-to-the-minute structures of glass towers, steel turrets, aluminium bricks: the Aviation Building, like a great hangar with a plane sticking out, the Electric Building, all burnished copper, the Marine Transport Building, streamlined buildings from Ford and General Motors. You could eat your way round the world at the foreign pavilions – the Italian one bore the carved motto 'Obey, Believe, Fight'. In the Amusement Park you could visit the penguin village, Jungleland, the midget colony, or the mechanised dairy. There was a winter sports resort with punctual snowstorms, and a facsimile of the Globe Theatre with 'staccato' performances of Shakespeare. You could watch the Olympic diving championships or Billy Rose's Acquacade, which featured Eleanor Holm and Johnny Weissmuller swimming in waltz time and attracted 40,000 visitors a day. Or you could enter Dali's Surrealist Fun House, a dreamworld shaped like an eye, where you encountered an eye with telephone-tipped lashes, and a seaweed-fringed piano with a chained woman as the keyboard.

Left, the Trylon and the Perisphere, symbols of the New York World's Fair, 1939. ANDRÉ DE DIENES

Above, spectators at the vast show 'Democracity', or City of Tomorrow, within the Perisphere. Industrial planner Henry Dreyfuss designed a decentralized city that was mechanized, efficient, and uncluttered, because everyone would have their homes outside in the countryside, 1939. KARGER

WOMEN SHOULD LOOK BEAUTIFUL

But do they in most sports?

'Of a list of some 25 sports in which ladies of today indulge with vehemence and passion – and also, it is noted with regret, in public – there are only nine in which they do not look utterly silly,' wrote Paul Gallico in a – presumably tongue-in-cheek – article in *Vogue* in 1936. 'The sports in which I will permit ladies to take part, in a mild and decorative manner, are archery, backstroke swimming, figure skating, riding, skiing, speed skating, aviation, shooting, and angling. And of these, shooting and skiing are on the doubtful list. Definitely interdicted are squash, tennis, track and field sports, boxing, wrestling, badminton, basketball, baseball, golf, fencing, hockey, breaststroke, handball, polo, rowing, and any other sports in which women stick out places when they play, wear funny clothes, get out of breath, or perspire. It is a lady's business to look beautiful. There are hardly any sports in which she seems able to do this.'

Regardless of what Paul Gallico thought, the craze for physical exercise affected all women. *Vogue* told you how to have fun getting fit in all sorts of ways: skating at the new ice rinks (complete with snack bars and dance bands), swimming, fencing, punching

medicine balls, and especially tap-dancing. Lillywhites opened a School for Figure Fitness with machines and massage belts, and Sir Alfred Beit had an electric gymnasium, whatever that was. Princess Jean-Louis de Faucigny-Lucinge and her friends made the Paris taxi strike the excuse for a craze of tandem riding. The latest thing was squash. 'Most new blocks of flats have courts now,' reported *Vogue* in 1937.

'Beauty, beauty,
To have it is everyone's duty
Every girl can get good looks
With the aid of one of our sixpenny books.
Beauty, beauty,
Just try a diet that's fruity
Full many a man has wooed a maid
On radishes and orangeade
With nuts to help him make the grade!
Three cheers for Beauty!'

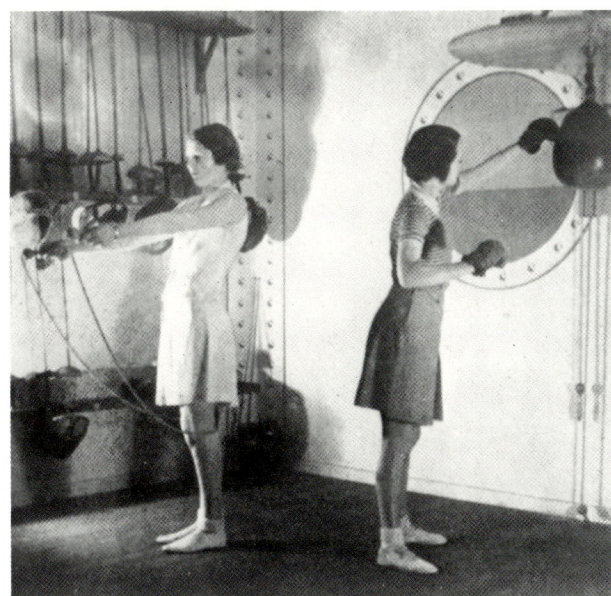

Facing page, below, Hermione Gingold as a 'Fitness Girl' in *The Gate Revue*, 1939, sang: 'Beauty, beauty . . .'

Top left, one of the sports of Paul Gallico's proscribed list: fencing, 1934

Top right, an American golf class practising to music, 1932

Above left, Princess Jean-Louis de Faucigny-Lucinge, wearing kneelength shorts, silk socks and sandals, beats the Paris taxi strike on a tandem, 1936

Above right, the gymnasium at Lansdowne House Club, 1936

Right, running on a roof track, 1934

Top margin, Erna Carise in one of her dances, 1933

ABOVE THE SNOWLINE

In winter society went off to ski or be seen on the slopes. St. Moritz remained the fashionable place to go, although *Vogue* discovered and popularised Kitzbühel, and the Prince of Wales took a holiday there. For Americans wishing to save themselves an Atlantic crossing, there was cross-country skiing in Yosemite, or a trip to the luxury resort at Sun Valley, Idaho, build by W. Averell Harriman at the cost of a million dollars, where you could ski one moment and swim in an outdoor hot springs pool the next. There were armchair lifts – you didn't even have to take off your skis – and six Austrian ski instructors to bring the Tyrol to the Wild West. Local cowboys and miners gaped, but half Hollywood, including Claudette Colbert, Dolores del Rio, Carol Lombard, and Loretta Young, booked in for the opening season in winter 1936.

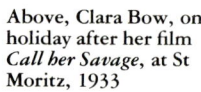

Above, Clara Bow, on holiday after her film *Call her Savage*, at St Moritz, 1933

Right, Gogo Schiaparelli, debutante daughter of the couturière, in Italy, 1938

Above right, Charlie Chaplin and larger-than-lifesize snow replica, St Moritz, 1932

Left, the Prince of Wales at Kitzbühel, the resort popularized by *Vogue*, 1935

Centre left, Princess Alexandra of Greece enjoying ski-joring, 1936

Above, the normally dapper filmstar Adolphe Menjou, wearing comfortable tweeds, with his wife at St Moritz, 1932

Top, the fearsome goggles and friendly flash of teeth of the guides of Davos, 1937

Top left, a happy group of skiers: the Hon Sandy Vereker, Mr Godfrey Winn, Miss Norris and Miss O'Roarke relax by the slopes, 1933

Above, Mrs Joseph Kennedy on the ice with Jean and Teddy, 1939

Right, M. and Mme Citroën pose for the camera in their stylish ski-wear, 1932

Top right, street scene at St Moritz, 1937

Above, tennis champion Suzanne Lenglen and film star Douglas Fairbanks at St Moritz, 1935

UNDER THE SUN

'The fashionable world is no longer centred at one spot, as it used to be at Cap d'Antibes,' wrote *Vogue* in 1931. 'The Riviera has become a fairground, bordering an endless road of countless curves along the sea, and is almost the most amusing place I know.' *Vogue*'s pages were full of personalities having fun under the sun, from Cap Martin to Toulon: Gertrude Lawrence at Monte Carlo, Michael Arlen ever faithful to Cannes, Chanel's 'self-service' entertaining at her villa La Pausa ... The most famous house in the South of France was Miss Maxine Elliot's villa at Cannes, which King Edward VIII took in August 1936. It had a 40-foot slide from the pool into the sea and was illuminated like Palm Beach at night.

The smart world loved the informality of this sunny playground. 'They find it novel to dress in workmen's jumpers, dance in nightclubs with sailors, dine at the Casino in shirt sleeves, and sit at night in the open-air movies

with maids, valets, and chauffeurs dressed exactly as they are.' In 1930 St. Tropez hit the limelight when the 'rampant theatricality' of the summer attire there became the gossip of the Riviera. For a season everyone wore dresses and tops fashioned out of the printed cotton handkerchiefs sold by Madame ('Ma') Vachon, while the amusing beflowered and beribboned straw hats made for diners at the quayside restaurant L'Escale by the owner's wife quickly became coveted. *Vogue* reported that the Prince of Wales bought a blue-and-white striped sailor's pullover in St. Tropez 'in which he looks very young and boyish'. Pyjamas were out and 'shorts have won the day'. The Princess Jean-Louis de Faucigny-Lucinge, the former Baba d'Erlanger, entertaining on her terrace, 'looks as chic as ever in her light backless swimsuit and the ribbon top-knot she has made so much her own'. It's the outdoor life round the pool from dawn till dusk, swim-

ming and sunbathing, and for Lady Mendl and her friends, standing on their heads.

Further afield, you might visit the Lido, which Elsa Maxwell turned into one of the smartest places around. Biarritz still had its devotees: the Duke of Westminster had an estate there and often entertained Mr. and Mrs. Winston Churchill. Cecil Beaton visited Palm Beach where socialites like Mrs. Harrison Williams and Mrs. Robert McAdoo took refuge from the New York winter among wicker chairs and hibiscus. And there was great cachet in being part of a houseparty, along with Mr. and Mrs. Reed Vreeland and Lord and Lady Brownlow, at Baron Rudolph d'Erlanger's minareted Arab palace at Sidi Bou Said in Tunisia. While escaping from the madding crowd, you could still find yourself photographed by *Vogue* photographers Horst and Hoyningen-Huené, who had also taken a house there.

Above, Marlene Dietrich on the Riviera, 1933

Right, Mr and Mrs Reed Vreeland in 'gay and unconventional dress' in the garden of Baron d'Erlanger's Tunisian palace, 1931. *Vogue* called her 'the last word in polished American chic'

Above left, Cecily Courtneidge at Monte Carlo, 1933

Above, Lady Louis Mountbatten, 1931

Left, Amy Mollison (*née* Johnson), Randolph Churchill, and Clare Luce, 1936

Far left, Chanel and Lucien Lelong on the Lido, 1930

Left, the ever-exhibitionistic Serge Lifar, limbering up as though a swimsuit were a leotard, 1933

Above, Grace Moore and Maurice Chevalier taking a dip on the Riviera, 1935

Left, Lady Diana Cooper, 1932

Above, Lord Portarlington indulging in the latest fitness fad, 1932

Above right, the Marquise de Casa Maury on the Riviera, 1930

Above right, Eunice, Jack, and Patricia Kennedy, 1938

Right, Princess Jean-Louis de Faucigny-Lucinge in a backless swimsuit 'and the ribbon topknot she has made her own', on her terrace at Cannes, 1936

A HOUSEPARTY

There is a chirping of birds, a quacking of swans in the moat. The curtains are drawn. There is always a certain coyness about the time you wish to be called in the morning. 'Pray, don't be too punctual, or do you prefer breakfast on a tray? If so, ring.' But, on a cold and frosty morning, I for one cannot resist the array of treacly sausages, the sputtering bacon and eggs, the haddock dish, and even the cold game looks tempting. There is a crackling of the fire in the hearth and the newpapers at the table: *The Daily Sketch,* with Wilhelmina Stich, the social gossip, and *The Times* with its official Court Circular.

Outside, the lawns are heavily dewed, and the thrushes hop about. Maybe it is planned that the day should be spent shooting; in which case, there is almost as much organization as for the production of a play. The chorus of beaters assembled look like mediaeval peasants in their strange assortments of garments. If it is hunting, a small leather flask of cherry brandy and a packet of sandwiches are on the chest or the hall table. The well-tied stock is stabbed with an enormous safety-pin, and the day yields a variety of sounds. The creak of the saddle, the crunch of the horses' hoofs on the gravel, and clop-clop on the roadside, the squelching in the mud, the hallooings in the distant coppice, and the other ghostly noises of the chase.

The meet is a vortex of gaiety. It is a particularly good day with crisp sunshine, and every one seems to be 'out'. 'Grand day, isn't it?' 'Laura Charteris promises well; she is coming out next year.' 'That's the famous Mrs. Tomlinson; she used to be the wife of a photographer on the Brighton Beach.' The hunt moves off: a minute later, pink-coated horsemen are hurtling over hedges, and dapper wine-glass-waisted ladies are dotted with mud. And what a big tea at the end of it all, with potted shrimps and boiled eggs, and a cold game pie on the sideboard!

Or perhaps the day has gone by in a rush of doing nothing, of waiting for the trunk-call to get put through and playing over and over the new record, 'Mediterranean Madness'. There have been short walks with twigs crackling underfoot. Or you have played a good game of golf, or, for Sachy's sake, motored in the neighbourhood to show him the various

Above left, a summer picnic at Cecil Beaton's, 1936

Above, at the Hunt Ball

Below left, Mrs Peter Thursby is ill

houses. You have hooted for the keeper to open the lodge gates and driven in the park land, and the deer have continued nibbling unperturbed. Or you have driven up through the courtyard and wandered through corridors, seeing eighteenth-century portraits in gold frames and heavy brocade curtains and busts on stands, and a neat fire in a grate; a bowl of hyacinths and a basket of wool.

The light fades early. The curtains are drawn – more logs piled on, and ladies sit around doing absurdly unnecessary petit-point work. 'The Wintheringtons were delighted we took Sachy over. The sound of the name Sitwell is magic to them, and he has a genius for saying the right thing and admiring their

particularly cherished treasures.' 'Really, I think the view at Wilton of the Palladian bridge and the Inigo Jones façade is the loveliest I know.'

The clock strikes, and there is a cocktail to impregnate one with energy enough to move from the depth of the sofa, to climb the stairs, and then there is the extravagance of soaking in a bath cloudy with salts. Then at dinner, the glow from the candlelight on the tables. A glittering island against the panelled gloom from which only the livery buttons are perceptible. Ladies in their apricot and tangerine coloured velvets.

The American ladies who have married into this existence seem very happy about their lot. The Hon. Mrs. Charles Winn [*née* van Heukelom] sits on shooting-sticks as though she had sat all her life on a shooting-stick. At Lismore, Lady Charles Cavendish [*née* Adele Astaire] wraps up in tweeds, but is getting acclimated to the cold. She takes guests and dogs down to the river which runs below the Castle and to the bogs for duck shooting; she has become a champion knitter and makes socks, sweaters and caps.

But why should I concentrate on other people's houses when I have a perfectly good one of my own? The existence that we lead at Ashcombe over winter week-ends is entirely different from that of summer. Who cares two hoots if it is wet? The fires are roaring, the

Left, guests at Lord Mandeville's shoot at Kimbolton Castle, 1938

Below, a sporting house-party

Text and drawings by Cecil Beaton, 1933

gramophone blaring. There are hundreds of summer snapshots to be stuck into albums, chestnuts to be roasted, and we have arrived complete with easels and palate. Lord Berners peers through the windows and paints the ilex-trees. Adele is taking up art and has her own water-colour box. Rex Whistler is making a design for an urn for Mrs. Courtauld. August-us John, nearby at Fryern, comes over for the day. We ride on the downs, the horses madly excited to be on such green turf. At one point, we are on the borders of Hampshire, Wilt-shire, and Dorset. We sightsee. Longleat, with one window for every day in the year, is not far, and there must be expeditions to see the beauties of Bath.. Or maybe, we decide to decorate a bedroom, so we all tramp upstairs and paint circus figures on the wall with magic effect. By the evening, the room is trans-formed. Rex has painted a fat lady, Gerald Berners a Columbine with performing dogs.

Dog days

'Surely no mother-love can equal the all-absorbing interest we feel in our pets,' wrote the Hon. Mrs. James Rodney in *Vogue*, 1932. Certainly one's canine friend was far too precious to leave at home: indeed you could tell who was lunching at the Colony by the dogs parked in the ladies' coatroom. Clara, the kindly attendant, catered for all doggy preferences: Elsa Maxwell's boxer Sager lunched on chopped raw steak, while Miss Taylor's poodle Quito was mad for Camembert. (Others took the regular *plat du jour*.) The Mitford sisters consented to appear in *Vogue* with their dogs Studley and Dominic, while the magazine's normally unsentimental Lesley Blanch confessed to spending 'hours of unparalleled emotion and joy' at Crufts.

Dogs headed the list of favourites, although many people went in for more original pets, such as ant bears, cockatoos, hummingbirds, and monkeys. Mrs. Morgan bought a monkey from an organ grinder and kept it in a 'sun-ray' cage. She also tried to keep a honey bear in her house in South Street but it cried all night and nearly clawed the bathroom door down. Captain Hammond's agouti slept in a corner of his bedroom. Stephen Tennant was fond of snakes, tortoises, and lizards, and Baroness Ceder-ström was devoted to her cranes.

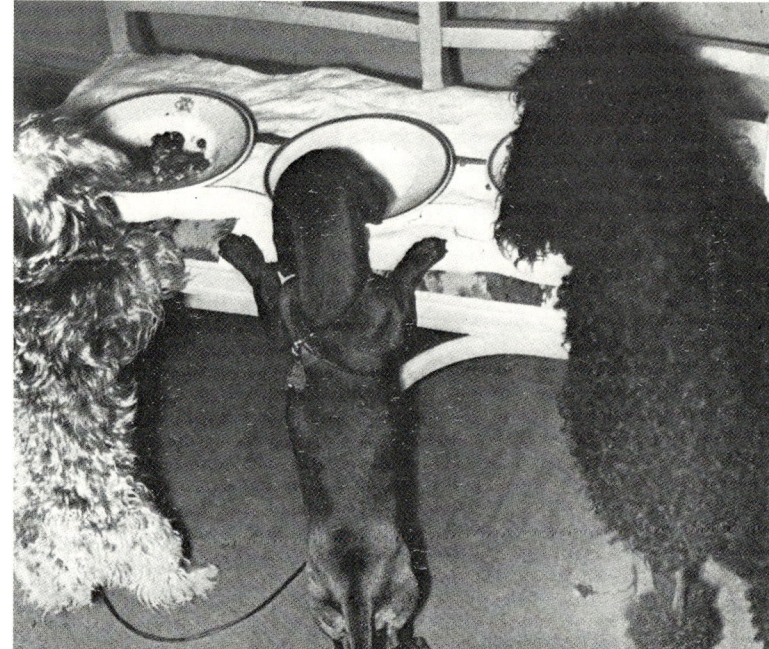

Left, Mrs Boardman's Sydney Silkie, Miss Chase's dachsund Quinta, and Quito, Miss Taylor's poodle, enjoy lunch at the Colony, 1938

Below left, Trinket, Miss Jenney's sealyham, begs for a titbit from Clara, the Colony's kindly attendant, 1938

Below, 'Of course I should make a reduction if you took the whole dozen.' Crufts, 1939.
FRANCIS MARSHALL

Above, the Hon Deborah and Jessica Mitford, youngest of Lord Redesdale's daughters, and their greyhound Studley and bulldog Dominic, 1936

Above right, 'I get a better coat on liver.' Crufts, 1939

Left, Afghan hounds, examples of elegant dogs, drawn by Vertès, 1935

Above, Viscountess Ratendone with her faithful sealyham, 1936

Above, the Hon Mrs Peter Rodd, otherwise Nancy Mitford, novelist and *Vogue* writer, with her bulldog Lottie, 1936

NURSERY LIFE

The Thirties saw great strides forward in child-care. In England, ante-natal clinics were established, and free milk in schools was introduced. There was Dr. Truby King to advise young mothers on the mysteries of mothercraft. And in certain progressive homes, even fathers were beginning to take an interest in their children. Influenced by psychologist John B. Watson's behaviourist experiments with infants and Bertrand Russell's injunction that children 'should not be forced to adjust to each other', parents called in the psychoanalyst at the drop of a rattle and moved house to be close to progressive schools. 'They are changing parenthood into one of the learned professions,' wrote *Vogue*. Among the questions perplexing these avant-garde papas were:

– Does it encourage Oedipus complexes to let children kiss their mothers goodnight?

– Should children be given nursery-size martinis so that they will not take alcohol too seriously?

– Should progressive children be shielded from believers in the stork and gooseberry bush?

'One of the catches of giving your child a radical education, of course,' wrote *Vogue*, 'is that he will find radicalism in any form highly congenial. Progressive school children tend to admire Surrealist paintings, Gertrude Stein, and the aims of the Communist International. One of the great unsolved problems of a progressive school in New York is reclaiming its children from the picket lines.'

But such fanatical ideas did not permeate into most English homes that *mattered*, and the tradition of nanny in the nursery, followed by Eton, Oxford, and the Guards, was still reassuringly adhered to.

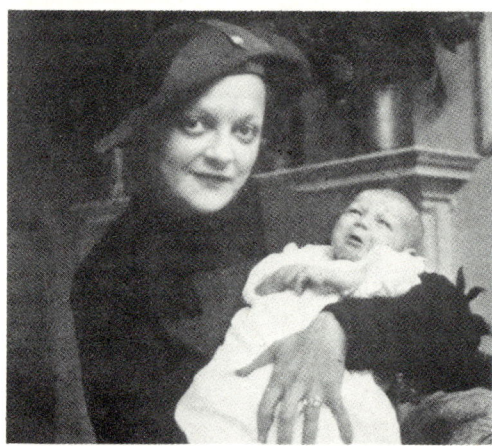

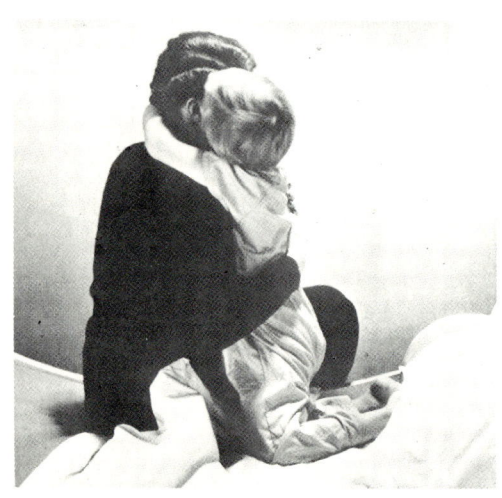

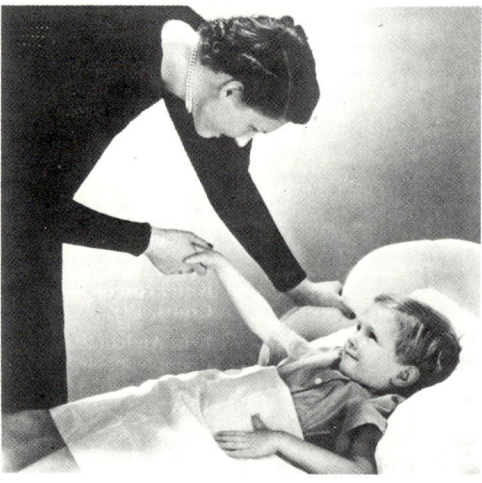

Opposite page: Top, Miss Leslie Howard, named after her film-star father, modelling a skirt from Fortnum and Mason, 1932. HORST

Centre, far left, an unusual shot of Marlene Dietrich: with her daughter Maria, 1932. STEICHEN

Centre, the Hon. W.H. Smith with his mother Viscountess Hambleden, 1932

Centre right, Sacheverell Reresby Sitwell, son of the poet Sachie Sitwell, 1935

Bottom, far left and centre, 'should you kiss your child goodnight or should you shake hands with him? How complicated the familiar task of bringing up a child has now become', 1937. Some extremist progressive fathers subscribed to the theory that a child who kissed his mother goodnight would end up with an Oedipus complex. STEICHEN

Bottom right, Raine McCorquodale, daughter of Barbara Cartland, absorbed in the business of answering some of her innumerable invitations to children's parties, with a little help and encouragement from Nannie Tuckett, 1933. Miss McCorquodale later became the Countess Spencer. JOHN HAVINDEN

Right, the Duchess of York and Princess Margaret Rose, 1931. MARCUS ADAMS

WAR!

Throughout 1939, Paris was preparing for war. Frenchmen were issued with gasmasks – 'although practically on-one knows how to put them on' – and beds of begonias were planted over bombshelters under the Champs Elysées. There was none of the frenzied jingoism of the Great War. 'The most noticeable difference in the women is that they have, with one accord, stopped wearing hats,' wrote *Vogue*. There were no *modistes* to make them.

There was no music, no dancing, and no movies after 10 o'clock. People dined early at Maxim's or the Coupole. 'There is a sudden need to feel friendliness warm about you . . . Everywhere the hot, dark, smoky rooms with windows closed and the waiters urging you to drink up before the police come to close the place, give night life a definite speak-easy flavour . . . Paris is in bed and asleep by midnight.'

The first air-raid warnings got everyone out of bed. Your maid put out your raid-shelter costume on a chair as she turned down your bed: slacks, sweater, tweed jacket, wool socks and gloves, sandals, flashlight, gasmask, keys, money. 'There is something deeply stirring about these democratic nocturnal *rendez-vous* with all classes huddled together,' wrote *Vogue*'s Bettina Wilson. Competition between concierges for the best cellar ran high; Miss Wilson found herself sneaking across the street, a traitor to her concierge, to one with light, card playing, and a gramophone – 'almost a café atmosphere'.

When Britain entered the war, *Vogue* advised readers to pass the time doing something useful – learning to cook, sew, or knit, or play an instrument, to pass the time, and to keep themselves up to scratch. 'It would be an added calamity if war turned us into a nation of frights and slovens . . . We deplore the crop of young women who take war as an excuse for letting their back hair down and parading about in slacks. Slack, we think, is the word . . . Determine then – in this European jungle – to dress for dinner.'

'News from the Mayfair front' reported a new purposefulness. 'It kills chichi deader than a doornail, finds better work for idle tongues than mere idle gossip.' Ladies doing National Defence work had to snatch half an hour to chat before going off to their all-night canteens

Right, 'the children who will not come home from school . . . Today with talk of a coming war heard everywhere, millions of Americans must stand firm in their determination that the folly of 1914–1918 shall not occur again.' Advertisement for World Peaceways, 1937

The Royal Family take up wartime duties, September 1939. Top left, Queen Mary passing between ranks of nurses. Top right, Queen Elizabeth at Aldershot. Above, the Duchess of Kent inspecting the St John Ambulance men. Right, the Duke of Gloucester with the Scots Guards

and ambulances. Playtime hours were now 5 till 11 instead of 8 till 2. The Berkeley held cocktail dances from 5 to 7. Theatres reopened. Bea Lillie in *All Clear* sang a naughty song about Hitler's secret weapon. You dined out in restaurants with cocktail-bar shelters, like L'Abri du Ritz or Prunier's, where you could get a Blackout Dinner for 10/6d, with oysters thrown in.

Vogue's Lesley Blanch saw the funny side of the phoney war in her article 'Crosstalk' – what the casual listener-in might hear in Mayfair in November, 1939: 'I quite thought she was a sandbag . . . Do you wear it over or under your gas-mask? . . . Poor lamb, her money was in neon-lights . . . Granny's been impossible since she got her stripe . . . Their shelter wouldn't even keep out leaflets . . . One or two lumps a week? . . . 'I'm trying to get *Grapes of Wrath* in braille to read in the train . . .'

Advertisements in Vogue

The early Thirties were lean years for magazine advertising: *Vogue*'s revenues reached their lowest in 1935. Manufacturers became more and more cautious about spending money on advertising space as the Depression caused markets to dwindle. However, after the repeal of Prohibition in 1934, advertisements for liquor, which had previously been illegal in America, became a lucrative fillip.

There were many more colour advertisements than during the previous decade. They were also more imaginatively designed and used more stylish typography. The *Vogue* illustrator Eric and tennis champion Helen Wills drew advertisements for shipping companies, and Covarrubias produced the Cubist-inspired 'American in Paris' design for Steinway pianos. Drawings were usually preferred to photographs, although yet another shipping line used a photograph by Steichen.

The Thirties was the age of famous campaigns such as 'That's Shell, that was!' and 'Guinness is Good for You'. But more often copy took the form of naive and pretentious prose that flattered your good taste and hinted that you understood the finer things of life if you smoked Weekend cigarettes or drove a Cadillac. Endorsements still sold things. Jean Harlow endorsed Lucky cigarettes, as did stars Madeleine Carroll, Robert Montgomery, and Metropolitan tenor Laurenz Melchior. Harlow was also happy to promote Lux soap, along with Mae West and Billie Burke. Ziegfeld Follies comedienne Fanny Brice was portrayed smoking Spud cigarettes, and Lady Howe apparently believed that 'the heart of a good cocktail is Gordon's Gin'.

Advertisements in *Vogue* included those for cigarettes, luxury cruises and travel, fashion and beauty products, alcoholic drinks and household goods. Campbell's soup, appearing every month without fail, represented a revolution in labour saving – as did such items as toasters, refrigerators, and food warmers. In 1932 the first advertisement for Kleenex disposable tissues appeared. As in the Twenties, advertisements for cars were some of the most striking, portraying monsters 'styled' with huge gridded radiators and massive headlights.

A few advertisements throw light on the ambiguous political awareness of the period. On the one hand, *Vogue* ran a travel advertisement for 'Germany, the land of hospitality' as late as August 1939. Yet as early as 1935 an organisation called World Peaceways used pictures of frightened children to try to make readers 'stand firm in their determination that the folly of 1914–1918 shall not occur again'.

Left, 'An American in Paris', painted for Steinway by Covarrubias, 1930

Above, 'a service to advertisers: Bruehl-Bourges photography and Condé Nast engravings', 1933

Right, Holeproof Hosiery, 'for the woman whose discriminative sense leads her instinctively to the beautiful'. Drawn by Erté, 1931

Driving was no longer in its hectic, dashabout infancy; it was regulated by pedestrian crossings, Belisha beacons, a highway code, and, after 1935, a driving test. Car advertisements dwelt not so much on freedom and escapism but emphasised luxury, comfort, dependability, and ease of handling.

Above, far left, the Pierce-Arrow convertible coupé 'with Free Wheeling', whatever that was, 1931

Above left, Cadillac, 'the supreme instrument of luxurious motoring', 1934

Below far left, the Ford V8, 1936. 'It is never any effort to drive a Ford – that is why it is so kind to your nerves and disposition'

Below left, 'as nimble as ethyl gasoline', 1931

Right, 'Wherever the car may be driven, it announces quietly, 'My people recognize the best'.' Lincoln Brougham, 1938

Cigarettes lent to both the men and women of the Thirties the required air of sophistication and self-assurance, and their advertisements reflect a new voluptuousness and sensuality.

Above, far left, a taste of the mysterious East: Gitanes Vizir, 1939

Above left, 'Do you inhale? Everybody's doing it! Seven out of ten inhale knowingly, the other three inhale unknowingly . . .
Luckies are less irritating than other cigarettes', 1936

Below, far left, 'These charming, well-groomed people found in Spud not only a lusty, limitless cigarette enjoyment . . . but also their imperturbable assurance of being 'mouth-happy'.' Spud cigarettes, 1939

Below left, Jean Harlow – 'not one cent was paid for her signed statement' – endorsing Luckies, 1932. 'It's a real delight to find a Cellophane wrapper that opens without an icepick'

Above right, Primerose cigarettes, 1931

Above, far right, 'Men and women who know a thoroughbred, whether it be a three-year-old or a cigarette' smoke Spud, 1932

Right, cigarettes to the fore: Weekend *goût anglais* cigarettes, 1935

In America, *Vogue's* advertising pages reflected the end of Prohibition with a prominent selection of liquor advertisements. Other luxury and labour-saving prepared foods were also well-represented.

Above, far left, 'the best apéritif is fresh air; the next best is Martini and Rossi Vermouth', 1934

Below, far left, 'There's no place like home for *the pause that refreshes'*. One of the earliest advertisements for Coca-Cola, 1934

Left, Chase chromium plates and electric buffet server, 1934

Right, 'Budweiser is naturally the choice of those who live life at its best'. Budweiser beer, 1933

One of the great strides in household design was the use of colour and co-ordination in such hitherto unlikely areas as bedroom and bathroom furniture, and even inks.

Above left, metal bedroom furniture in a choice of eight colours by Simmons, 1938

Below, far left, 'the Pannier adds a final touch of line and colour that completes the style motif of your bath ensemble'. Whitney clothes hampers, 1931

Below left, 'Church Coloured Toilet Seats have taken the country by storm', 1930. They were available in 'lovely pastel shades and richly lustrous sea-pearl tints'

Above right, 'Fold a silken rainbow across the foot of your bed'. Palmer comfortables, 1930

Top, far right, 'We domesticate the typewriter': decorative covers by Remington, 1930

Centre, far right, 'the newest in smart letter writing is color'. Carter's Jewel Inks, 1932

Below right, Cannon towels, 1933

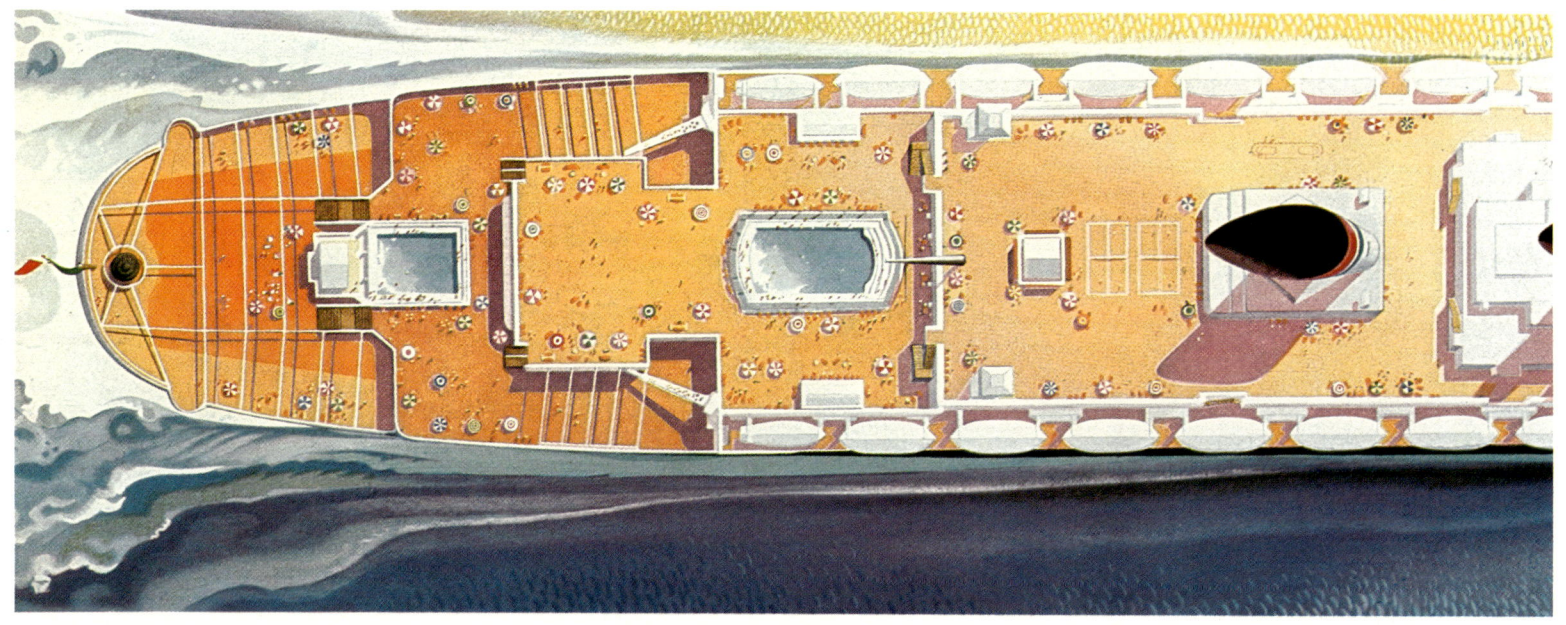

Cruising was the fashionable way to travel, and the emphasis was on luxury. Ships competed with each other, offering dining rooms with roll-back domes which opened to the sky, beauty salons, and pre-release talkies.

Above left, '48 hours out . . . and they left home in a blizzard.' A Lido crossing on the Italian Line, 1937

Below left, Hawaii via Matson Line, photographed by Steichen, 1934

Above right, 'more and more, it is the travel fashion to go South by sea . . .' To Miami and Florida with Clyde-Mallory Lines, 1930

Above, far right, dining under the stars on a Grace Line liner, 1936

Below right, dancing on the glass floor aboard the French Line ship *France*, 1931

Below, far right, 'Otchkotch? . . . Oochkooch? Better to be guilty of mis-pronunciation than travel with anything less than the best trunk in the world,' 1930

INDEX

Abbott Girls *55*
Abdication, the 12, 20, 24
Abdy, Lady 17, *33*, 57, *59*
Alajálov *71*, *126–7*
Alexandra, Princess , of Greece *134*
Ambassadeurs 55, 56, *59*
American School of Ballet 74
Amphytrion 38, 83, 87
Anglesey, Lady 36
Anna Christie 99
'Anything Goes' 8
Après-midi d'un Faune, L' 62
Arlen, Michael 136
Arlen, Mrs Michael 62
Armstrong, Louis 68
Art Deco 112, *113*
Ascot 42, *46–7*, *48*, *49*
Ashcroft, Peggy 83
Ashton, Frederick 73, 74, *75*
Askey, Arthur 14
Asquith, Margot *see* Oxford, Lady
Astaire, Adele *see* Cavendish, Lady Charles
Astaire, Fred 8, 80, *80*, *81*, *94*, *105*
Astor, Lady 8, 47
Auden, W.H. 8, 18, 83, *90*

Bagnold, Enid 93
Bailby, Leon 62
Baillie-Hamilton, Mrs 36
Baiser de la Fée 74
Baker, Josephine 79
Bal Tabarin *52*, *56–7*
Balanchine, Georges 74, *74*, *77*
Baldwin, Stanley 20
Baldwin, Mrs Stanley 37, 47
Ballet Rambert 75
Ballets de Monte Carlo 44
Ballets Russes *72*, *73*, 74, *74*
Bandwaggon 15
Bankhead, Tallulah *83*, 85, 100
Baranova, Irina 73
Barnes, Binnie 85
Barretts of Wimpole Street, The 85
Basie, Count 14, 68
Basil, Colonel de 74
Bat night club 53, *53*
Bauhaus, Dessau 18
Bax, Arnold 70
Baxter, Warner 100
Baylis, Lilian 73
Beaton, Cecil 8, 17, 18, 20, 28, *36–41*, *41*, 62, 64, 78, 83, 94, *115*, 129, 136, 138
Beatty, Lady *114*
Beau Geste 94
Beaverbrook, Lord 20
Bedaux, Charles 20
Beecham, Sir Thomas 44, 70
Beerbohm, Max 44
Beistegui, Charles de *113*
Beit, Sir Alfred *132*
Bel Geddes, Norman 122, 130
Bell, Vanessa 24
Bennett, Constance *63*, *100*
Bérard, Christian 57, *63*, *64*, *73*, 74
Bergner, Elisabeth 14, *88*, 89
Berkeley Hotel 45, 144
Berkshire Festival 71
Berlin, Irving 68, 80
Berlin 14, *59*
Berners, Lord 36, 70, 75, 139
Bernstein, Henry 56

Bernstein, Mme Henry *62*
Best, Edna 97
Biarritz 136
Big Apple (dance) 14, 68
Blanch, Lesley 18, 68, 84, 100, 140, 144
Blandford, Marquess and Marchioness of 47
Blue Angel, The 99
Blue Lantern 53
Blue Train 45
Boeuf sur le Toit *54*, 55, 57
Bon Viveur 53
Bourdet, Édouard 57
Bow, Clara *134*
Bowen, Elizabeth 8, 18
Boyer, Lucienne 56
Braque, Georges *106*
Brave New World 18, 90
Brecht, Berthold 14
Breuer, Marcel 112
Brice, Fanny 146
Brick Top's 55
British Union of Fascists 8
Brittain, Vera 92
Britten, Benjamin 70
Brownlow, Lady *25*, 136
Burke, Billie 146
Byng, Douglas 78

Cabaret *54*, 55
'café society' 12, 53
Cage, John 70
Cagney, James 94
Caldwell, Erskine 8
Calthrop, Gladys 89
Camargo Ballet 73
Cannes 118, 136
Cap d'Antibes 136
Carisbrooke, Lady 89
Carise, Erna *133*
Carnet de Bal, Un 99
Carpentier, Georges 56, *59*
Carroll, Madeleine *103*, 146
Casa Maury, Marquis and Marquise de 53, *89*, *137*
Casteja, Comtesse Alexandre de *116*
Castlerosse, Lady 89
Cavalcade 83, 85
Cavendish, Lady Charles 138
Cecil, Lord David 92
Cederström, Baroness 140
Central Park Casino 61
Chamberlain, Neville 18
Chanel 8, 17, 74, *103*, 136, *137*
Channon, Chips 40
Channon, Lady Honor *30*
Chaplin, Charlie 12, *13*, 36, 37, *94*, *134*
Charlie's Bar 36
Chase, Edna Woolman 24
Chase, Ilka 85
Chevalier, Maurice *137*
Chez Georges 56
Chirico, Giorgio de 8, *106*, 109
Christie, John 70
Churchill, Diana 61
Churchill, Randolph *136*
Churchill, Winston 136
Churchill, Mrs Winston 61, 136
Ciro's, London 53
Ciro's, New York 61
Citadel, The *88*, 93
Citroën, M. and Mme *135*
City Lights 99
Clair, René 99
'Cliveden Set' 8
Cochran, C.B. 11, 78, 89, 112

Cochran, Jacqueline *124*
Cockburn, Claud 8
Cocteau, Jean 8, 15, 18, 57, 84
Colbert, Claudette 94, *96*, *100*, 134
Cold Comfort Farm 12
Colefax, Sybil *114*, 116, 117
Colette 116, *116*, 117
Colman, Ronald 100
Colony 140, *140*
Colombo, Russ 60
Connie's Inn 53
Cooper, Lady Diana *34*, 36, *36*, 41, *89*, *137*
Cooper, Gary 100, *102*, 113
Cooper, Gladys 28
Copacabana 118
Corn is Green, The 85
Cornell, Katharine 85, *86*
Corrigan, Douglas 122
Coster, Howard and Joan *31*
Cotton Club 53, *55*
Country Club 54
Coupole *144*
Courtneidge, Cicily 136
Covarrubias, Miguel *16*, *77*, *105*, 106, *106–7*, 118, 146, *146*
Covent Garden 24, *43*, 44, 70, 71, 73
Coward, Noel *13*, 44, 53, 78, 83, *84*, 85, 88, *89*
Crawford, Joan 12, *13*, 15, *94*, *98*, *100*
Cronin, A.J. 93
Crosby, Bing 60, 68
Crowninshield, Frank 12, 53
Crufts 140, *140*, *141*
cruising 17, *128–9*, *156–7*
Cunard, Emerald, Lady 70, 73, 89
Curie, Eve 35, 67
Curzon cinema 53, *54*

d'Abernon, Lord 47
Dali, Salvador 8, 18, 56, 74, *105*, *106*, 108, 109, *109*, 110, *110*, 130
Dali, Mme 110
Davis, Bette 100
Day, Frances *89*, 129
Day-Lewis, Cecil 8
De Marcos, the *80–1*
Depression, the 8, 11, 18, 62, 83, 112, 146
Dérain, André 74, *75*
Derby, the 42
d'Erlanger, Baba *see* Faucigny-Lucinge, Princess Jean-Louis de
d'Erlanger, Baron Rudolph 136
d'Erlanger, Mrs Leo *34*
Dermoz, Germaine 88
Design for Living 83, *88*
Detroit Symphony Orchestra 71
Diaghilev, Serge 73, 74
Dickson, Dorothy 89
Dietrich, Marlene 12, *12*, 17, *94*, *95*, *136*, *142*
Disney, Walt 94, 97, *105*
Dolin, Anton 73
Dorchester Hotel 37, *37*
Dorn, Marion *115*
Dorsey, Tommy 68
Douglas, Lord Alfred 85
Dreyfuss, Henry *131*
Dubonnet, André 116
Duchin, Eddy 53, 61, 68

Dudley, Countess of 24
Duff, Lady Juliet 41, *89*
Duff, Michael and Joan 41
Du Pont, Mrs Richard 122
Durbin, Deanna 94
Duvivier, Julien 99

Earhart, Amelia 17, 122, *124*
Eddy, Nelson 94
Eden, Mr and Mrs Anthony 89
Eden End 83
Edward VII 20
Edward VIII 11, 12, 20, *20*, *21*, *23*, 26, 71, 113, 134, *134*, 136
Einstein, Albert 8
El Morocco 53, *54*
El Patio 53
Elizabeth, Queen 12, 20, 24, *25*, 26, *26*, 27, *143*, *144*
Elizabeth, Princess 24, 26, *26*, 27
Ellington, Duke 14, 53, 68
Elliott, Maxine 136
Embassy Club 45, 53
Erickson, Carl (Eric) *64*, *118*, 146
Ernst, Max 18
Erté *147*
Escholier, Raymond 57
Eton 42, *42*
Evans, Edith 83

Façade 73
Fairbanks, Douglas 12, and Mrs *63*, *135*
Fairbanks, Douglas Jr 6, *103*
fancy dress balls *62–5*
Fascism 8
Faucigny-Lucinge, Princess Jean-Louis de *34*, *132*, *133*, 136, *137*
Faulkner, William 90
Fellowes, Daisy (the Hon Mrs Reginald) 17, 57, *64*, 116
Featherstonhaugh, Major and Mrs 47
Feyder, Jacques 99
Fields, Gracie 78
Flagstad, Kirsten 71
Flanner, Janet 8
Fleming, Peter 129
Florence's 56
Flynn, Errol *103*
Fokine, Michel 44, 74
Fonda, Henry 8, *102*
Fontanne, Lynn 60, 83, 87, *105*
Fonteyn, Margot 74, *75*
For Whom the Bell Tolls 18
Formby, George 78
Forres, Lady *42*
Fouquet's 55, *59*, *59*
Fowler, John *114*
Foyle, Christina 92
Franco, General 8
Frank, Jean-Michel 56
Frankenstein 94
French Without Tears 83
Freud, Sigmund 8
Furness, Thelma, Lady 11, 20, 28, 47

Gable, Clark 94, 100
Gallico, Paul *132*, *133*

Gandhi 37
Garbo, Greta 12, 94, *94*, 99, 100
Geiger's Hungarian Orchestra 37
George V 11, 14, *20*
George VI 12, 20, *24*, 26
Georges Cinq Bar 56
Gershwin, George 62, 80
Gibbons, Stella 12
Gielgud, John 83, *86*
Gingold, Hermione *132*
Giraudoux, Jean 83
Glyndebourne 70
Goddard, Paulette 99
Goering, Hermann 41
Goetz, Ray 61
Gone With The Wind 18, 99, *100–1*, *100–1*, 130
Goodman, Benny 14, 68, *105*
Gordon, Ruth 88
Graham, Martha 77, *77*
Gramont, Elizabeth, Duchesse de *45*, 57
Granard, Earl and Countess of 47
Grand Ecart 55
Grand Hotel 85, 94
Grand National 46
Grande Illusion, La 99
Grant, Duncan 129
Grant, Mark Ogilvie 67
Grapes of Wrath, The 18, 144
Greene, Graham 12, 18, 90
Greville, Mrs Ronnie 36, 38
Gropius, Walter 18, 112
Guernica 18
Guitry, Sacha 99

Hambleden, Viscountess 142
Hammett, Dashiel 90
Handful of Dust, A 92
Handley, Tommy 15
Happy Hypocrite 44
Harlow, Jean 94, 100, 146, *150*
Harriman, W. Averell 134
Harrison, Rex 88
Haugwitz-Reventlow, Countess 14, *30*, 89
Hayes, Helen 85, 87
Hays Code 94
Headfort, Lord and Lady 89
Hearst, Mrs 61
Heifetz, Jascha 113, *115*
'Heigh Ho' 94
Hellman, Lillian 85, 92
Hellzapoppin 99
Hemingway, Ernest 8, 18, 68
Henley 42
Hepburn, Katharine *82*, 97, 100, 122, *124*
Herbert, David 41
Hiller, Wendy 83, 97
Hitchcock, Alfred 97
Hitler, Adolf 8, 12, 15, *17*, 18, 20, 41, 57, 85, 86, 144
Hobson, Valerie 97
Hoctor, Harriet 78
Holm, Eleanor 130
Holm, Hanya 77
Hopkins, Miriam 12, *100*
Hornby, Lady Veronica 40
Horst 17, 28, 136
Hot Mikado 69
Houseman, John 86
Housman, Laurence 85, 87, 92

Howard, Leslie 94, 97
Howard, Miss Leslie *142*
Howe, Lady 146
Hoyningen-Huené 17, 28, 136
Hughes, Howard 122
Humphrey, Doris 77, *77*
Hutchinson, Leslie 68
Hutton, Barbara *see* Haugwitz-Reventlow, Countess
Huxley, Aldous 8, 18, 90
Huxley, Julian 37

I am a Fugitive from a Chain Gang 94
I, Claudius 96
Idiot's Delight 86, 94
International Brigade 8
Invisible Man, The 99
Irwin, Pee Wee 68
Isherwood, Christopher 8, 18, 83
It Happened One Night 94
ITMA 15
Ivy restaurant 53

Jamaica 118
Jasinsky 73
jitterbug 14, 68
John, Augustus 40, *41*, 139
Johnson, Amy 122, *122*, 136
Johnson, Philip *112*
Jouvet, Louis 83

Kahn, E.J. 77
Kapurthala, Prince and Princess Karam de *59*, 67
Kennedy, Eunice, Jack and Patricia *137*
Kennedy, Jean and Teddy *135*
Kennedy, Joseph 15
Kennedy, Mrs Joseph 15, *135*
Kent, Duchess of 11, *11*, 89, *144*
Kent, Duke of 11, 89
Kern, Jerome 80
Kiki *54*, 55
King, Dr Truby 142
King Kong 94
Kitzbühel *134*, *134*
Klee, Paul 18
Knoblock, Edward 38, 89
Kochno, Boris 63, 75
Korda, Alexander 97
Koussevitzsky, Sergei 71

Laborde, Charles 57
La Croë *21*, *22*, *23*
Lady Vanishes, The 97
Lambert, Constant 70
Lambeth Walk 14, *15*, 78
La Môme Moineau 57
Lang, Fritz 97
Laski, Harold 8
Laughton, Charles *84*, 97
Laurencin, Marie 8
Laver, James 94
Lavery, Lady 47
Lawrence, Gertrude 83, *84*, 136
Laye, Evelyn 89
Le Corbusier *113*
Left Book Club 8
Léger, Fernand 61, *106*
Lehar, Franz 78
Lehmann, Lotte 70, 71
Lehmann, Rosamund 18, 90
Leigh, Mrs Claude 89
Leigh, Vivien 94, 97, *101*

Lelong, Lucien *137*
Lelong, Mme *33*
Lenglen, Suzanne *135*
Lichine, David 74
Lido, Venice 17, 73, 136
Lifar, Serge 38, *38*, 62, 74, *137*
Lillie, Beatrice 38, *38*, 41, 78, 84, 144
Lindbergh, Anne Morrow 122
Little Caesar 94
Little Foxes, The 83, 85
Livingstone, Belle 54
Loch Ness Monster 18, 40
Lombard, Carole 96, 134
Lombardo, Guy 68
London 8, 24, 36–9, 42–5, 53, 59
Londonderry, Lord and Lady 89, 122
Longchamps 47, 56, 59
Lonsdale, Frederick *61*
Lonsdale, Lord 47
Look on the Dole 83
Lopokova, Lydia 73
Lord, Pauline *88*
Lords 42, 42
Losch, Tilly 38, *38*, 78
Louise, Anita 129
Love on the Dole 83
Luce, Claire *80*, 136
Luce, Clare Boothe 63, 85, 87, 89, *92*, 122
Lunt, Alfred 60, 83, 87, *105*, 117
Lygon, Lady Mary *33*
Lynn, Olga 41, 70

M 97
McAdoo, Mrs Robert 61, *118*, 136
MacArthur, Charles 68
McCorquodale, Raine *142*
Macdonald, Jeanette 94
MacDonald, Ramsay 8
Machine Infernale, La 84
McMullin, John 8
MacNiece, Louis 8, 83
'Mad Dogs and Englishmen' 83
Mainbocher 11, 20, *21*, 117
Maltese Falcon, The 90
Mandeville, Lord *139*
Mann, Thomas 93
Mannes, Marya 77
Mansion Club 61
Mar and Kellie, Earl and Countess of 47
Marais, Jean *88*
March, Fredric *100*
Margaret Rose, Princess 24, *26*, 27, *143*
Marina, Princess *see* Kent, Duchess of
Markova, Alicia 74
Marquand, John P. 93
Marsh, Sir Edward 89
Marx Brothers 94
Mary, Queen 12, 20, *144*
Massey, Raymond 85, 87, *88*, 89
Massine, Leonide 74, *74*
Masson, André *110*
Matisse, Henri 18, 74, *106*, *111*
Matthews, Jessie 78
Maugham, Liza 38, *38*
Maugham, Syrie 15, 38, 67, 112, *114*, 117
Maugham, W. Somerset 18
Maxim's 55, 144

Maxwell, Elsa 12, 41, 61, 62–3, 63, 64, 66, 67, 136, 140
Me and My Gal 14, 78
Melchior, Laurenz 71, 146
Mendl, Lady 12, 17, 41, *41*, 57, 62, 64, *65*, 66, 113, 136
Menjou, Adolphe *134*
Merman, Ethel *61*
Messel, Oliver *51*, 66, 67, 78
Metropolitan Opera 70–*1*, 71
Mies van der Rohe, Ludwig 18, *112*, 112
Mildmay, Audrey 70
Milford Haven, Marquess and Marchioness of 89, 129
Millar, Gertie *see* Dudley, Countess of
Miller, Gilbert 85, *89*
Miller, Mrs Gilbert *61*, 89
Miller, Glenn 68
Miranda, Carmen 79
Mistinguett 62, 63, 64
Mitchell, Margaret 18, 100
Mitford, Hon. Deborah and Hon. Jessica *141*
Mitford, Hon. Nancy 8, 90, *141*
Mitford, Hon. Unity 8
Moholy-Nagy, Laszlo 18
Mollison, Amy *see* Johnson, Amy
Molyneux 11, *18*, 59, *117*
Monopoly 18
Monseigneur bar 53
Montagu-Douglas-Scott, Lady Alice, *see* Gloucester, Duchess of
Monte Carlo (nightclub) *50*
Montgomery, Robert 94, 146
Moore, Grace 41, *41*, 61, 71, *137*
Moppès, Maurice van *58*
Morgan 57
Morlay, Gaby *62*
Morley, Robert 85, 87
Mortimer, Raymond 92
Mosley, Sir Oswald 8
Mountbatten, Lady Louis *25*, *29*, 113, *114*, *136*
Mountbatten, Lord Louis 113, *114*
Mourning Becomes Electra 84
Mumford, Lewis 117
Murder in the Cathedral 83
Mussolini, Benito 17, 57

Nast, Condé *61*
National Defence 18, 144
National Velvet 93
New York 8, 14, 15, 18, 53, 59, 60–*1*, 62, 129, 136, 142; World's Fair 18, 130
New York Philharmonic 71
Nichols, Beverley 89
Nicolson, Harold 8, *92*
night clubs 45, 50–5
Night and Day 61
Night Must Fall 85
Night at the Opera, A 99
Nijinska, Bronislava 74
Nijinska, Kyra 78
Nikitina, Alice 38
Ninotchka 99
Norfolk, Duke of 24
Novello, Ivor 44, 78, 89

Oberon, Merle 96, 97
Obolensky, Prince Serge *15*, *61*, 63
ocean liners 17, 126–9, *156–7*

Olivier, Laurence 83, *84*, 86
Olympic Games 1936 15, 41, 99
Ondine 83
O'Neill, Eugene 84
Onyx Club 68
Orwell, George 8, 18
Oscar Wilde 85, 87
Osterley Park Georgian Ball 66, 67
Owens, Jesse 15, 130
Oxford, Lady 8, *32*, 36, 37, 38, 89
Oxford Union 8
Ozeray, Madeleine 83

Paget, Lady Elizabeth 41
Palm Beach 136
Pam Am clippers 17, 122
Paravicini, Mr and Mrs Vincent 89
Parents Terribles, Les 84, 88
Paris 11, 52, 54, 55, 56–9, 62, 84, 144
Patou, Jean 9, *120*
Pauly, Rosa 71
Pearson, Lady *see* Cooper, Gladys
Pegler, Westbrook 97
Penguin books 18
Persian Room Club 53
Picasso, Pablo 18, 60, 106, *106*
Piguet 18
Pirandello, Luigi 15, 84
Plunket, Lady 89
Polignac, Comtesse Charles de *116*
Polignac, Comtesse Jean de 56
Polignac, Marquis de 41
Poniatowski, Princess 67
Pons, Lily 56, 57, 71, *105*
Porter, Cole 8, 61, *61*, 62, 63, 80, 113, *115*
Porter, Mrs Cole 61, *63*
Porter, Katharine Anne 92
Portland, Duke and Duchess of 47
Poulett, Lady Bridget 89
Powell, William *100*
Power, Tyrone 94
Priestley, J.B. 83, *90*
Printemps, Yvonne 56
Prisoner of Zenda, The 99
Private Life of Henry VIII, The 97
Private Lives 83, 84
Prohibition 53, 146, *152*
Pru, Edwina *see* d'Erlanger, Mrs Leo
Public Enemy 94
Putnam, George 17
Pygmalion 97

Quaglino's 53
Queen Mary 17, 128–9
Queensberry, Lady 89

Rain 98
Rambert, Marie 73, *75*
Ratendone, Viscountess *141*
Rathbone, Basil 86
Rattigan, Terence 83, *90*
Ravensdale, Lady 37
Ray, Man 17
Rebecca 97
Reed, Carol 97
Reinhardt, Max 8
Reith, Sir John 14, 37

Rembrandt 97
Renoir, Jean 99
Reunion in Vienna 60, 83
Rhett, Alicia *100*
Riabouchinska, Tatiana 74
Riccio, Comte 41
Richardson, Ralph 83, 88
Riefenstahl, Leni 99
Rio, Dolores del 134
Ritz Hotel *18*
River Club 60
Rivera, Diego 18
Riviera 8, 17, 118, 136
Robert, Louise *100*
Robertson, Doris *115*
Robinson, Bill 69
Robinson, Edward G. 94
Robson, Flora 84, 97
Rodd, Mrs Peter *see* Mitford, Hon. Nancy
Rodgers and Hart 80
Rodney, Hon. Mrs James 140
Rogers, Ginger 8, 80, *81*, 94, *105*
Romilly, Esmond and Giles 8
Roosevelt, Mrs 12, 85
Roosevelt, President 14
Rose, Billy 130
Rosse, Lord 67
Roxburgh, Duke and Duchess of 47
Roy, Pierre 8, *10*, *109*
Ruhtenberg, Jan *112*
Russell, Bertrand 142
Rutland, Duchess of 36

Sackville-West, Vita *92*
Sadler's Wells 73
St Moritz 17–18, 134, *134–5*
St Tropez 17, 136
San Marco restaurant 45, *51*
Sanctuary 90
Savoy Hotel 45; – Grill 53
Sayers, Dorothy 90, 92
Scandals 60
scavenger hunts 63
Schiaparelli, Elsa 11, *16*, 17, 20, *35*, 59, 67, 68, *95*, 109
Schiaparelli, Gogo 67, *134*
Seldes, Gilbert 15
Selfridge, Gordon 89
Selfridges 11, 24
Sert, Misia 61, 62
Service, Reggie 68
Shaw, George Bernard 84, 97
She Done Him Wrong 99
Shearer, Norma 96, 113
Sheridan, Clare 37
Sherwood, Robert 83, 85, 86, 94
Silly Symphonies 97
Simpson, Mrs Wallis 11, *11*, 12, 15, 20, *21*, *22*, *23*, 113, 116
Sitwell, Edith *39*, *91*
Sitwell family *39*
Sitwell, Osbert 38, *39*
Sitwell, Sacheverell *39*, *92*, 138
Sitwell, Mrs Sacheverell *39*, *142*
Smith, Dodie 44, 89
Smith, Lady Eleanor 36
Smith, Lady Pamela 38
Smith, Hon. W.H. 142
Snow White 97
Sorel, Cécile 57
Spanish Civil War 8, 18
Spencer, Earl 36
Spender, Stephen 18, 83
Spry, Constance 66
Stalin, Joseph *16*

Stamboul Train 90
Stanley, Lady Maureen 97
Star Dust 61
Steichen 8, 17, 28, 146
Stein, Gertrude 56, 142
Steinbeck, John 18
Stewart, James 8
Stokowski, Leopold 60
Strachey, John 8
Strathmore, Earl of 26
Stravinsky, Igor 74
Stroheim, Erich von 99
Sullavan, Margaret *100*
Sullivan, Maxine 68
Sun Valley 134
sunbathing 15
Surrealism 108–10, 129, 130
Sutherland, Duchess of 118
Sutro, Alfred 38
Sutton Club 61
Swanson, Gloria 45
Sweeny, Charles 89
Sweeny, Mrs Charles *31*, 89
'Sweet and Lovely' 60
'swing' 14, 68

Taillefer, Germaine 62
Taylor, Robert 94, *102*, *105*
Tchelichew, Pavel 8, 77, *110*
Teagarden, Jack 68, *68*
television 15
Tempest, Marie 89
Temple, Shirley 12, *13*, 94, *105*
Tennant, Stephen 140
Testament of Youth 92
*There'll Always be an England' 18
They Won't Forget 94
Thirty-nine Steps, The 97
Thompson, Dorothy *105*
Thompson, Sylvia 42–5
Thorndike, Sybil 85
Time and the Conways 83
Times, The 138
Tonight at 8.30 44, 83
Too True to be Good 84
Top Hat 80
Toscanini, Arturo 60, 70, 71
Toumanova, Tamara 73, *75*
Tracy, Spencer 94
transatlantic flights 122
travel 17–18, 118–29, 136–7
Triumph of the Will, The 99
Trocadero 53
Trojan War will not take Place, The 83
Tucker, Earl 53
Twentyone ('21') Club 53

Vachon, 'Ma' 136
Vallee, Rudy 68
Valois, Ninette de 73
Vanderbilt, Mrs Fair 60
Vanderbilt, Mr and Mrs Reginald *28*, *120*
Vaughan Williams, Ralph 70
Vereker, Hon. Sandy *135*
Vertès 55, *57*, *141*
Vic-Wells Ballet 73, 74
Victoria, Queen 20
Victoria Regina 85, 87
Vienna Philharmonic 57
Vilmorin, Louise de 58
Vionnet 48
Vogues of 1938 104
Vreeland, Mr and Mrs Reed 117, 136, *136*

Wadsworth, Edward 129
Wagner, Walter *104*
Walbrook, Anton 88
Waldorf-Astoria 18, 61, 63, 94
Wales, Prince of *see* Edward VIII
Wall Street Crash 8
Waller, 'Fats' 68
Walter, Bruno 57, 70
Walton, William 70, 73
War of the Worlds, The 14
Ward, Mrs Dudley *115*
Ward, Penelope Dudley 83
Warrender, Sir Victor and Lady 89
Watson, John B. 142
Waugh, Evelyn 8, 18, 92
Waves, The 60
Weidman, Charles 77, *77*
Weissmuller, Johnny 130
Weldon, Sir Anthony 118
Welles, Orson 14, 86, 87, *105*
Wells, H.G. 14, 37, 89, *90*
West, Mae 94, 99, 146
Westminster, Duke of 136
Westminster, Duchess of *25*
Whigham, Margaret *see* Sweeny, Mrs Charles
Whistler, Rex 27, 44, 85, 89, 113, *139*
White Horse Inn 85
Whitney, Mrs Cornelius Vanderbilt 122
Whitney, Mrs Henry Payne 61
Wiborg, Miss Hoytie 60
Wigman, Mary 77, *77*
Wilding, Dorothy *28*
Williams, Cootie 14
Williams, Emlyn 85
Williams, Mrs Harrison 61, *61*, *118*, 136
Willingdon, Lord 89
Wills, Helen 146
Wilson, Bettina 144
Wilson, Jack 89
Wimborne, Viscountess 24
Windsor, Duke and Duchess of *see* Edward VIII and Simpson, Mrs W.
Winn, Godfrey 89, *135*
Wizard of Oz, The 99
Woizikovsky, Leon *75*
Wolfe, Thomas 90
Women, The 85, 87
Wong, Anna May 40, *40*
Woolf, Virginia 18, 60, 93
Woolley, Monty 61
Words and Music 83
Wynyard, Diana *88*, 97

Years, The 93
York, Duke and Duchess of *see* George VI and Elizabeth, Queen
Young, Loretta 134

Zerbe, Jerome 54
Zoppola, Countess Edith di *118*

ACKNOWLEDGEMENTS

My greatest debt for this book is due to *Vogue*'s publisher Condé Nast and its editors of the Thirties, Edna Woolman Chase (the American Editor-in-Chief), Alison Settle O.B.E. and Elizabeth Penrose (Britain), and Michel de Brunhoff (France). Between them they were responsible for commissioning the artists, writers, and photographers who gave the magazine its distinctive character during the decade. I would also particularly like to thank Alex Kroll, for his guidance and assistance at all times during the making of *The Thirties in Vogue*. Among the numerous other people who contributed in various ways, I would especially like to mention Rupert Kirby, for assisting with the design, and Bunny Cantor, for her tireless help with the research.

I should like to dedicate *The Thirties in Vogue* to my parents.

C.H.